Tell Better Stories for Kids

Revise Your Chapter Book

Write a Book for Kids Series

Darcy Pattison

Tell Better Stories for Kids: Revise Your Chapter Book

© 2026 Darcy Pattison. All Rights Reserved.

Previously published as Novel Metamorphosis: Uncommon Ways to Revise, 2nd edition by Darcy Pattison, © 2012, print. © 2016, ebook. Darcy Pattison.

No part of this book may be reproduced in any form or by any electronic or mechanical means including information storage and retrieval systems without permission in writing from the publisher, except by a reviewer, who may quote brief passages in a review.

Mims House
1309 S. Broadway
Little Rock, AR 72202

MimsHouseBooks.com

Publisher's Cataloging-in-Publication Data
Names: Pattison, Darcy, author. | Larson, Kirby, foreword author.
Title: Tell Better Stories for Kids: Revise Your Chapter Book / by Darcy Pattison; foreword by Kirby Larson.
Description: Little Rock, AR: Mims House.
Identifiers: ISBN 9781629443263 (paperback) | 9781629443317 (ebook)
Subjects: LCSH Fiction--Technique. | Fiction--Authorship. | Manuscripts--Editing. | Manuscript preparation (Authorship) | BISAC LANGUAGE ARTS & DISCIPLINES / Writing / Fiction Writing | LANGUAGE ARTS & DISCIPLINES / Editing & Proofreading | LANGUAGE ARTS & DISCIPLINES / Writing / Authorship
Classification: LCC PN162 .P38 2026 | DDC 808.3--dc23

Permissions

"The Wonderful World of Words," adapted from Marsteller, Bill. The Wonderful World of Words: Memoranda and Speeches of Bill Marsteller 1951-1972. Marsteller, Inc. 1972. Used by permission from Harold Burson, Burson-Marsteller, Inc., New York, NY

Contents

Write a Book for Kids Series v
Tell a Better Story - Re-Thinking Your Chapter Books ix

1. Why Tell Better Stories? Why Revise? 1
2. The Novel Inventory 13
3. Scenes 25
4. Plot 33
5. Characters 43
6. Choosing Details 67
7. Language 73
8. Setting 85
9. Depth 91
10. Your Revision Plan 99
11. Homework 103
12. Recommended Reading 105
13. APPENDIX A: I Don't Want an Honest Critique 121
14. APPENDIX B: Group Manuscript Evaluation Form 125

About the Author 127

Write a Book for Kids Series

"Look, Mom, a skwy-skwayper."

My two-year-old daughter was showing off her vocabulary. Where had she learned about skyscrapers, triangles, and newts? From children's books.

I raised four children to become readers, and in the process, I fell in love with children's literature. For years, I have studied and written, written and taught about how to write children's books. In many ways, it's the same as any lesson on writing. Good literature is good literature, regardless of the age of the audience. In the *Write a Book for Kids Series*, I'm teaching how to write good literature, and how to bring it to market and find the right readers. Sometimes, there are special notes about writing for different ages. For example, the developmental growth of a sense of humor affects how you write humor for kids. But by and large, these are books about writing great stories.

The books in the series can be read in any order, depending on your needs.

- *Write a Kid's Picture Book: Create Heartfelt Stories* will

help you with the short, 32-page picture books for the 0-10 year-old audience.
- *Start a Kid's Novel: Develop Story Ideas for Children's Chapter Books* helps you take a story idea and develop it into a full novel.
- *Writing a Novel for Kids: Prompts to Create Fun, Heartwarming Chapter Books* is about the process of writing going from a discussion of titles and subtitles, to a deeper look at character, plot, and subplots.
- *Tell Better Stories for Kids: Revise Your Chapter Book* helps you revise novels intended for 7-14 year olds. It helps you transform your novel from good to great.
- *Publish a Kid's Book: Find Surprising Success Self-Publishing* is meant to help you bring books to market yourself.

Pick up the books that you need when you need them.

British writer Walter de la Mare said, "I know well that only the rarest kind of best can be good enough for the young."

These books are in hopes that we will produce '...only the rarest kind of best..." for the kids who read our books.

Thanks to all the kids who have ever let me share a story with you. You have enriched my life with your enthusiasm and joy in a story well told.

Darcy Pattison
Mims House Books

Write a Book for Kids Series

Write a Kid's Picture Book: Create Heartfelt Stories

Start a Kid's Novel: Develop Story Ideas for Children's Chapter Books

Write a Book for Kids Series

Writing a Novel for Kids: Prompts to Create Fun, Heartwarming Chapter Books

Tell Better Stories for Kids: Revise Your Chapter Books

Publish a Kid's Book: Find Surprising Success Self-Publishing

Tell a Better Story - Re-Thinking Your Chapter Books

by Kirby Larson

I began writing nearly twenty years ago. I have had plenty of experience reworking manuscripts, trust me. So why did I sign up for Darcy Pattison's Novel Revision Retreat in 2004?

Blame it on my grandmother. A story she had told me about her step-mother homesteading in eastern Montana spurred me to write my first historical novel. I'd spent three years doing research and had a solid manuscript drafted. Solid but not singing.

Coincidentally, a friend told me about Darcy's workshop and I signed up. But Darcy is so darned bossy! She sent out in-depth instruction sheets detailing what we were to bring to the workshop, including a copy of the manuscript printed out in 8–point font. 8–point font? Insanity. What was this woman thinking? I was ready to ask for my money back.

Deep down, however, I knew I needed this workshop. I saw my novel as a love letter to a grandmother I adored, so nothing less than perfection would do. Grumbling only slightly, I packed up my laptop, my manuscript—including that version in 8–point font—and headed off for the workshop.

Tell a Better Story - Re-Thinking Your Chapter Books

It didn't take long for me to realize that while I had had plenty of experience rewriting, there was a lot yet to learn about revising. Working through Darcy's exercises, I re-visioned my book. I wrote feverishly that summer weekend and in the two months following. In October 2004, I sent the manuscript to Delacorte. Ten days later, the editor called to make an offer. In September 2006, *Hattie Big Sky* was published and in January 2007, it won a Newbery Honor award, given by the American Library Association to books that demonstrate a distinguished contribution to children's literature.

Is it all because of Darcy's workshop? No, of course not. But if writing is 10 percent vision and 90 percent revision—well, you do the math.

So, congratulations for having completed a manuscript—no small task. And congratulations for caring enough about your work to spend time re-visioning it. You are in good hands with Darcy, even when she asks you to print out your manuscript in 8– point font.

Kirby Larson
www.kirbylarson.com
www.hattiebigsky.com

Chapter 1
Why Tell Better Stories? Why Revise?

We're going to talk about revising your manuscript. Our goal is to tell better stories.

Why take all those words you just wrote and mix them up again? Because good writing is revised writing. Robert Frost has said, "I have never been good at revising. I always thought I made things worse by recasting and retouching. I never knew what was meant by choice of words. It was one word or nothing."

I wish we were all like Frost, able to write once and never have to revise; but few of us have that genius for words. Most of us would have to agree with Vladimir Nabokov, "I have written—often several times—every word I have ever published. My pencils outlast their erasures."

Or Dorothy Parker, "I can't write five words but that I change seven."

Or John Kenneth Galbraith who jokes, "There are days when the result is so bad that no fewer than five revisions are required. In contrast, when I'm greatly inspired, only four revisions are needed."

Or Truman Capote: "I believe more in the scissors than I do in the pencil."

I think Frost is overruled by his peers.

But what about us? Do we believe that revising is the only way to write well?

I once taught a teacher in-service about the importance of revising and started by reading them the quotes above. Each teacher nodded in agreement: revising is important. Over the next six hours, each revised a piece of writing six times, using six different strategies.

At the end, one teacher remarked, "Wow, I didn't know revising would make so much difference!"

We give lip service to the idea of revising. We want to have revised well. But we don't want to revise. It is essential that you revise.

There. That's all my wisdom in one fell swoop. Revise.

You're convinced? Good. Ah, but you don't know how? That's what this book will help you do.

Who Am I?

Answer #1

I am not an agent, an editor, or a high school English teacher. I'm not trying to find a manuscript to buy, to make money off of, or to nitpick grammar. I am a writer who struggles to write stories just as much as the next person struggles. I am in the trenches, turning out drafts of stories, revising those drafts and making submissions. I know the pains, the struggles and the triumphs, and that's the source of the exercises and strategies presented here. I know what one small insight, one small change can make in a story.

I am also a writing teacher. For over twenty years, I've taught kids, teachers, and fiction writers, and they are the other source of these exercises and strategies. Their questions have made me think about what is essential and how to communicate those things in ways that will make a real difference.

Answer #2

The 2004 Whidbey Island, Washington, Novel Revision Retreat almost didn't happen. The organizer thought she had enough people to attend, so she didn't do a lot of advertising. At the last minute, one person learned they were to receive a child to adopt. Another was sick. For various reasons, participants dropped out, until there were only seven left.

The organizer called: "Do you still want to do the retreat?"

Yes. Many years ago, I settled for myself the question of how important it is to speak at places where there were only a few in the audience. For me, there are no little people, no little places. Each person still scheduled to come to the retreat was important. For some reason—I don't know why—I care about the writers who carry both their manuscripts and their hopes to a retreat. I care passionately. I believe in each manuscript, each writer.

The retreat went on, even though yet another attendee was caught in a delayed international flight back home and was so jet-lagged that she couldn't pay much attention. Only six people fully participated in the retreat, the smallest number I've ever had. One of those writers was Kirby Larson. After the retreat ended, she went home and revised (she did the hard work!) and sent off her manuscript. It sold within ten days. Ten days! Kirby Larson's book, *Hattie Big Sky* (Delacorte, 2006), went on to win the 2007 Newbery Honor award, given by the American Library Association to books that demonstrate a distinguished contribution to children's literature. Wow!

Your story matters and you matter. That's what I care about. For me, there are no little people, no little places.

Is This Book is For You?

This book is especially designed for writers who have completed a draft of a novel. If you haven't finished one yet, read and learn and do any exercises that look helpful. But when you've finished a full draft, come back, ready to dig in and work.

The book is also designed for writers who will actually work through the exercises. Over and over, I hear Retreat participants say, "If I was just reading this at home, I wouldn't actually do it, but it really works." These exercises only work if you do them. Intellectual knowledge isn't the same as hands-on experience.

Think, plan, dream. Revise.

Congratulations!

From here on, I'll assume that you've finished a full draft of a novel. So, before we go any farther, I want to stop and say to you, "Congratulations!" Many begin; few finish. To have come this far—you've done an amazing, wondrous thing. Yes, there's more work to come, but we writers need to stop and celebrate each major step along the way. In the Retreat, we go around and shake every other person's hand and tell them, "Congratulations." It's important to celebrate. Congratulations!

Before We Start

First Drafts

Frankly, I don't care how you get your first draft written. Of course, there is the controversy about should you write from an outline, or should you just start out writing and see where the characters take you. Advocates of each method will expound long and hard about the values of each. I recognize that there are valid answers in both approaches. In the end, you must produce a first draft; that's not my concern here.

Instead, I'm fascinated with what happens next. Once you know the basic characters, plot, setting—the basic story—then the question you answer as you write changes.

No longer are you worried about, "What is the story?"

Now, you should focus on, "What is the most dramatic way to tell this story?"

Dramatic presentation of a story means that the reader is hooked and can't put it down; the reader is emotionally impacted; the characters stay with the reader for years to come; the reader laughs, sighs, weeps.

Do you want to just tell a story? I don't. I want to tell a powerful story. Revisions are the messy route toward powerful stories. I can't tell you how to revise your story; in fact, when I present this as a Retreat, I never tell someone how to revise their story. Instead, I ask you to look at your story in different ways, apply various strategies of revisions, and tell your story, your way. You are in control and will make all the decisions yourself.

There is only one decision you can't make: you can't decide not to revise.

The Heart of My Story

Before you revise, though, you should take time to think about what is the heart of the story for you. Why did you write this story and not a different story? If you had to change everything except one thing—what is that one thing? Write a paragraph about what is the heart of this story FOR YOU?

• • • • • • •

What to Expect

We're going to be looking at some basics of writing a novel and then move into some more advanced areas. I can't teach you to write well in a single book. But I can point you in the right direction and toward resources that can help. Here, at the beginning, you are all full of hope. Hope that someone—finally—will be able to help you on your novel. That's what this book is designed to do. Before we begin, there are some ground rules.

One way of describing the learning process is in terms of competencies.

Stages of Learning
  Unconscious Incompetence
  Conscious Incompetence
  Conscious Competence
  Unconscious Competence

First is the level of unconscious incompetence (you don't know and you don't know that you don't know). A step up is learning that you are incompetent in an area (you don't know, but you know that you don't know). When you move to a level of competence, it is usually because you've been consciously working on the skills and knowledge needed for competence (You know and you know that you know). The final step is unconscious competence (you know, but you don't know that you know), in which skills and knowledge are internalized and almost automatic.

The most important thing you learn from this book may be that you are incompetent in one area. It makes for strange conversations.

Writer: That book taught me that I'm really, really bad at dialogue.
Friend: Then—why are you smiling?
Writer: Don't you get it? Now that I know I'm bad at dialogue, I can study and work and learn to write better dialogue. This is an important step in my writing career.

It means you have to find resources to learn that area, and you may have to spend time practicing the skills needed. Competence is a hard-won prize that only comes with lots of study and practice.

Comfort Levels

One other caution about this book. Since you've finished a complete draft of a novel, I consider you Gifted & Talented. I've talked with Gifted & Talented Teachers about how their students learn. When these students learn something new, they go through a stage where they are very uncomfortable about what is happening. They are unsure of what to do next. Some students get mad when something doesn't instantly work right—possibly for the first time in their lives.

While using this book, you may feel some of this uncertainty, this discomfort, as you stretch to learn new ways of working. I want you to know this up front: you may feel frustration, despair, anger—things way out of your comfort zone. This is a normal result of learning something new. What you must not do is give up or refuse to try. Hang in there for the whole book! By the end, you will be feeling much better, I promise.

Focus on Your Story

You must also translate everything in the book to your story. A good analogy is the color palette of a certain piece of art. One piece may have mostly pastels in the palette, just like your story may have a narrow overall range of conflict and emotion. Another painting might have the entire spectrum of colors from white to black and every color of the rainbow, just like a novel may deal with birth, death and a wide spectrum of emotions between these. You can't say one palette is better than the other; you can only say that it works for this painting or it doesn't. Always remember to translate everything in terms of your story.

Be Open to Change

Look back to the previous page where you wrote something about "The Heart of My Story." Decide now that you will not change the one thing you wrote there, but be willing to change everything else. Critiquers may say that you need to change this or that, but from your point of view, that one thing is why you wrote the story. It's okay to put that one thing off limits: Cling to those "Heart" sections because they are essential for you. But if you cling to one thing, you must realize that it has ramifications throughout the story and you must be willing to change anything and everything else. Everything. Nothing else can be held back.

Try to Be Objective

Finally, let me caution you that I have certain biases in the type of stories I like and so do your other critiquers. The only one who gets to be particular about what they like is the acquiring editor, who backs up his or her opinion with cold, hard cash. The rest of us need to try to be objective about subject matter, plotting, characterization. There are many different ways to characterize effectively and the point isn't to get you to do it my way, but to do it effectively. I hope you'll find a new and great way to do it! This book is designed to point out this or that element which needs work, give examples of how others have dealt with this, and then let you try writing until something works.

Typical Critiquers

In critique groups, I find that writers/readers have different styles of critiquing.

Grammar Witch: This person always finds the punctuation, spelling, and grammar mistakes; I'm grateful for them, because fixing what they notice is easy.

Line Editor: This person rewrites lines by omitting words, moving things around, or just rewriting a sentence here or there. I appreciate the efforts of this person, but I don't always do what they suggest. I consider everything they suggest. But I also take into consideration the voice of the piece; sometimes, the Line Editor has put the sentence(s) into his or her voice, destroying the rhythms of my voice. Sometimes, the Line Editor's suggestion to omit a word is right on. Or, they've noticed that I've repeated "whirl" ten times in this chapter, and they are right, I should drag out a thesaurus. Overall, my attitude towards these critiquers is one of caution.

Big Picture Critiquer: The hardest critiquers to find are those who can look at the shape of the overall story and see holes in the story logic, where the pacing is off, where the characters are flat, where dialogue is boring, etc. For me, these are the most valued critiquers. This is why I always want my critiquers to read the entire story at one time, even if it's a rather long novel.

Sometimes, this type critiquer is the quietest in the bunch and you have to listen carefully. For example, once a group went over my WIP (work-in-progress) with enthusiasm, but as I was leaving, one person said casually as we were walking out the door, "Really, though, I don't think you'll get it published until you resolve the parent-child relationship."

Whoa! That was a great Big Picture Comment, but it was made casually, almost apologetically. Fortunately, I realized the importance of that comment, the most valuable comment of the hour's critique. Listen for the small voices.

Under-Confident Critiquer: This person looks at a

published writer and says to themselves, "Oh, gee, I can't say anything to them because they are published and they know everything." Sorry, but publication of one book doesn't mean you write the next one perfectly. Even writers with 100 books out need honest feedback from honest readers. I avoid these critiquers because they refuse to give an honest opinion.

Using the Book in Groups

When I teach the Novel Revision Retreat, I structure it so that each person gets maximum feedback on his or her novel. Participants are divided into groups of four: they exchange manuscripts before the retreat and everyone reads all the manuscripts from their group. Using the Group Manuscript Evaluation Form in Appendix B, they evaluate each story. After each session and its accompanying exercises, groups meet to discuss each manuscript in turn. I suggest that you try to find some way to duplicate this type of group interaction.

This book can help you revise, but having outside readers is valuable, too. The maximum benefit comes when a group works through these exercises together. My suggestions for the group discussions will get you started, but remember to let the manuscripts dictate what you discussions. It's best to cover all the chapters in a short time period so participants will not be tempted to begin a revision before they finish the exercises. That would give you a moving target, a novel that is constant flux and difficult to evaluate. The weekend retreat works well, but you could accomplish this by meeting several intensive weeknights, too.

Appendix A, *"I Don't Want an Honest Critique"* is a plea for group members to understand the pain, uncertainty, yet hope that occurs before, during and after a critique session.

Recommended Introductory Reading

This book assumes that you have some basic competencies. These books are an excellent review of these competencies. When I do a Novel Revision Retreat, participants are asked to read these as homework before attending. If you can master what these two books discuss, your manuscripts will get you into the top 1% of the stories written. It's getting into the top .001% of manuscripts that actually get published that the rest of this book is about.

Browne, Renni and Dave King. *Self Editing for Fiction Writers*. New York: William Morrow Paperbacks, 2004

Lukeman, Noah. *The First Five Pages*. New York: Fireside, Simon & Schuster, 2000.

Chapter 2
The Novel Inventory

At this point, there are two manuscripts: the one in your head and the one you put down on paper. And they aren't the same! You must find out what you actually wrote, not what you thought you wrote. What do you actually have in this draft? That's what this revision strategy helps you find out.

Start a revision notebook, either paper or digital, for your novel. Write this on the first page:

Date of Inventory:_____
Name of Novel:_____
Length:_____

Plot and Emotional Inventory

1. Two line inventory - first line. You're going to write an inventory of your novel in a notebook, or in a file on your computer. Number each chapter and allow two lines per chapter. On the first line allowed for a chapter, in one—and only one—sentence, write the main action of that chapter; this is about the outer conflict going on. If there are subplots going on, you may use a second sentence for the subplot. In the margin, put a checkmark at the beginning of each chapter if the chapter contains conflict.

2. Second line. On the second line for each chapter, in one—and only one—sentence, write the main emotions of each chapter; this is about the inner conflict going on.

Example from *The Wayfinder* by Darcy Pattison (Greenwillow/Harpercollins). In this example, the emotions are in italics.

_____1. Apprentice Wayfinder Winchal Eldras escorts Mayor Porter through the dangerous f 'giz (heavy fog) to the most important party of the year. *Win is confident in his Finding skills.*
_____2. Win's family deals with the f 'giz and he tries to protect his little sister, Zanna. *Win has affection for his sister, Zanna.*
_____3. Win searches for Zanna, who is lost in the fog, but is too late to save her from falling into the Rift. *Fear paralyzes Win, so he can't stop her fall.*
_____4. The grief-stricken Win finds his way home by following the Finder's Bell. *Win is confused, in shock and in denial.*

In your revision notebook, write out the chapter inventory for your book.

Climax and Epiphany Questions

Answer these questions in your revision notebook. Keep the answers short and focused.

BRIEFLY TELL THE MAIN CONFLICT OF THE STORY:

. . .

Briefly tell how this main conflict is resolved by the climax of your story:

How many pages does your climax cover?

Who is present at the climax?

Where does the climax take place?

What is the final conflict?

Does your character experience an epiphany? What?

Does your character see him/herself differently at the end? How?

Strongest Chapters

Look back at the summaries of the chapters. Circle the chapter numbers of the strongest five (5) chapters. That is, the chapters in which the action is the strongest, the outcome changes something drastically for the characters, or the emotions are the strongest. (Or, hopefully, all three!) Now, rate the chapters from 1-5, with 1 being the strongest chapter, 5 the least strong of these five.

(Note: This is arbitrary, but it works well to mark about five strong chapters in a novel that is up to about 40,000 words. If you have a longer novel, mark more chapters in proportional amounts. 60,000 words, mark seven or eight; 80,000 words, mark ten; etc.)

Characters

Looking ONLY at the first five manuscript pages of your novel, write down everything you know about the main character.

(Note: If you have a first chapter where the main character is not introduced, do this for the first section that introduces the main character. This could be perfectly reasonable: think of the first chapter of *Holes*, by Louis Sachar, which is about the lizards.)

The Box Test for Scenes

A scene is a section of a story in which action slows down and you give the reader a moment-by-moment experience. A scene starts with a character who wants something, who has a goal. Of course, we're nasty fiction writers, so the character's goal is thwarted over and over so that the scene ends in disaster. To use agent Donald Maass' mantra: Conflict on every page! Afterwards, there's a moment for the character to have an emotional reaction to the scene's events, before s/he decides to act again, sending the story into a new scene.

Directions for Box Test

The Box Test will easily tell you if you are writing in scenes or not. Go through a chapter or two of your manuscript and draw a box around each scene. Each scene should have a clear opening, middle and conclusion, even if it is compressed into in a single paragraph, or a single sentence. The scenes should have actions at their heart, not just thinking or emotions. The boxes may be connected by transitional elements that won't be in a box.

What if you go through a chapter and can't find a section that seems to hang together? Events happen, but there doesn't seem to be a section with a distinct opening, middle and ending that leads to a new scene. Then, you may not be writing with scenes, so just move on to the next exercise for now and wait for the Scenes chapter.

Answer these questions about your scenes:
    Did you write in scenes?
    What did you notice about your scenes by doing the Box Test?

Overall Inventory

In your revision notebook, answer these questions.

What I like most about this draft of the novel is...

Pretend you are a salesman and have ten seconds to sell this book. Summarize the story in one sentence:

Find and mark in your manuscript passages that best illustrate the following:
    Best characterization in my novel is found on page_____.
    Best dialogue in my novel is found on page _____.
    Best setting in my novel is found on page_____.
    Best imagery in my novel is found on page _____.
    What else did you notice about your story while doing this inventory?

Debriefings

Each section will end with a debriefing. Take time to look back over the information and exercises and evaluate where your novel stands on this topic. Later, you will use these as you plan your first revision.

Inventory Debriefing

After doing this inventory, what surprised you about your novel? (Good or bad?) Look back at page 2, where you wrote about your novel's Heart. Do you still agree that this is the Heart of your story? Why or why not? Write a new Heart for your story if you need to.

What are your problems, concerns, or worries about this novel?

Group Session 1: Discuss Inventories

Gossip Time

One of my favorite moments of editor interaction was when I was revising my novel, *The Wayfinder*. The editor called and we chatted about the ongoing revisions.

Then, she asked, "By the way, who is Win's father?"

The main character's father was never stated in the story, just implied. I told her some of the backstory of the novel. She responded that it was perfect and the implications of that revelation meant this and that.

I suddenly realized: we were gossiping about my characters!

Wow! Characters who came out of my imagination were so interesting, that we were gossiping about their lives. What a cool thing!

Group sessions should be like that. Gossip about characters from your novels. Ask the trivial, but fascinating things you've been aching to find out. Enjoy the feedback from someone who has read your entire novel.

Get Acquainted

If you've done as I suggested, your group has already exchanged novels and read through them before you started this book. In some ways, you'll know the others in your group pretty well because of their novel, but it's still important to take a few minutes to get acquainted and just chat.

Set up any group procedures that you feel you need. For example, sometimes, it's helpful to appoint one group member as timekeeper to make sure that each novel gets equal time.

Discuss each novel in turn. Depending on your time schedule, discuss an overview of each novel: writing style, characters, plot, setting, imagery.

Other Inventory Tools

The Novel Inventory provides one good way to evaluate your manuscript overall, especially when you want to diagnose the weak areas of a draft. Here are two other great ways to see the big picture of your story.

Spreadsheet Plotting

Some writers like to keep a running inventory of their story by doing Spreadsheet Plotting. Choose your favorite spreadsheet program and open it. I totally ignore the line numbers at the left. Choose any line at the top and type in the novel's title. Skip down a couple rows and set up columns. One advantage of this strategy is the flexibility to chart areas that you need to look at. Typical columns include these:

Act. This helps track the act to which this scene belongs.

Chapter. This helps divide the story into chapters.

Headlines. This isn't a summary of the scene's events, but headlines of main events of the scene with emphasis on how it affects the main character(s).

Time. Time of year, time of day. This helps track the passage of time and keep events in order, or deliberately out of order for flashbacks.

POV or Characters present. This column helps ensure

that each character has a proper amount of exposure. Use the colored initials for each character for at-a-glance evaluations.

Setting. This tracks movement. Typically, some settings recur throughout the novel, and this tracks when they are repeated.

Action. Similar to Headlines, but with a different function. The Headlines puts the event in context of the main character, while the Action can be more specific or give a context. For example, one Headline reads, "Jamie sees a special greyhound for the first time." The Action column reads, "The Greyhound Adoption Services presents information at the summer fair."

Pulse. This highlights the emotional tension driving this scene. It is the engine, the question, the tension that keeps the reader turning pages.

Words. To track the manuscript's length, add a column for the number of words/chapter and set up the spreadsheet to keep a running total.

The beauty of a spreadsheet is the ability to sort. If, for example, I want to know how many times, I've had my characters visit Baby Beach, I click the top of the Setting column. It sorts the entries into alphabetical order and I see that they've only been to Baby Beach twice, once in Act I and once in Act III. It tells me that I might need to send them there sometime in Act II. Note: Of course, this means that as you enter information on the spreadsheet, you must use consistent terminology, or the sorting feature won't work.

Overall the Spreadsheet Plotting gives you an ongoing Inventory for a look at the Big Picture of your story.

The Shrunken Manuscript

One of my teaching goals is to make things visible whenever possible. Seeing the Big Picture of a novel is hard, though, because it's spread over 100+ manuscript pages. How do you see what is so spread out? With the magic of today's computers, there's no reason for it to be so spread out!

Tell Better Stories for Kids

Instructions for the Shrunken Manuscript Strategy

1. Open your manuscript in your word processor. Take out the chapter breaks, so there is no white space between chapters.

2. Single space the entire mss.

3. Reduce the font of the mss until the mss takes up about 30 pages, usually 8 pt or 6 pt. This is arbitrary, of course, but I find that I can see about 30 pages at a time. It doesn't matter if the font is readable; you're trying to shrink the mss so you can mark certain things and you won't be reading it but evaluating how these things fit into the big picture. If your mss runs over 40,000 words, you can try putting it into two columns in order for it to fit into 30 pages. If your mss is over 50,000 words, you may need to divide it into two sections and evaluate 30-shrunken pages at a time.

4. Use a bright, wide marker and put an X over the strongest chapters identified the Inventory.

5. Lay out the mss pages on the floor in about three rows of ten. (Adjust layout to your page count, of course.)

6. Stand back and evaluate. What does this visualization tell you about the revisions needed? One typical thing to notice is that the strong chapters occur near the front and the end of the story: this type manuscript has the dreaded Sagging Middle. Sometimes there is strong scene in the middle, but it's very short: the proportions are off here, with the majority of the text in the weaker chapters.

• • • • • • •

Darcy Pattison

For more on how to see your manuscript by making the Shrunken Manuscript, see a series of videos on eight ways to mark your manuscript. Included are instructions for evaluating scenes, narrative arcs, plotting, story points (beats), emotional arc, emotional story points, and dialogue.:
https://IndieKidsBooks.com/shrunken-manuscript

• • • • • • •

While the Spreadsheet Plotting could tell you how the strong chapters are spread out, this strategy is good for seeing the proportions of text in each strong chapter, a very different thing. You can use the Shrunken Manuscript to evaluate anything that you want to visualize across the novel: settings where two characters interact, the percentage of dialogue, places where you repeat a certain setting, places where the theme is made obvious, etc. Often novelists mark several things at once with different colored markers, or by putting sticky notes on the manuscript.

Comparing the Inventory Strategies

The main difference is that the Shrunken Manuscript is more visual, while the Spreadsheet Plotting is text based. The novel inventory is designed to show weak areas in general, while the other two strategies can help pinpoint problem areas.

Advantages of the Novel Inventory

The Novel Inventory is a general diagnostic tool that cuts across many areas of concern at once. As a general tool to direct your revision efforts it's helpful. It also forces you to evaluate the manuscript you wrote, not the manuscript you thought you wrote.

Advantages of Shrunken Manuscripts

Shrunken manuscripts are a visual look at the overall shape of a story. They are particularly good at showing the proportions of a manuscript that deal with your issues. Because you mark/highlight entire chapters or passages, you can see—at a glance—how much space deals with your issue. Often, it's not enough just to mention Character X; instead, the reader needs fully developed scenes that take place over extended time in order for X to be memorable. Spreadsheet plotting doesn't show this as easily; you can include a column on the number of pages, but it's not visual.

It's also easy to see multiple issues at a time, by using different color highlighters, or sticky notes. For example, you can check on interactions between X & Y, X & Z, etc. and see if they are spaced where you want and if they last long enough.

Advantages of Spreadsheet Plotting

On the other hand, spreadsheet plotting allows you to check the actual content of scenes/chapters. For this reason, it's easy to scan a column of plot points and see if the narrative arc builds over the course of these actions. Or, scan the column of emotional points and see how the emotional arc builds. Try sorting columns: as long as you use consistent terminology, you can check, for example, how many times you place scenes in a haunted house.

For me, these complimentary methods of looking at the overall shape of a novel are the most helpful tools.

Chapter 3
Scenes

Stories have a structure, such as a 3-act structure. On a smaller level, the building blocks of each act are the scenes, where characters and plot interact. In the Inventory, I asked you to put boxes around a scene. Often, writers discover that they are not using scenes at all, or their scenes are weak. Either way, we'll be working on strengthening your scenes.

What is a scene?

A scene is a section of a story where the author slows down and gives us a detailed blow-by-blow account of what is happening. Scenes cover a short amount of time and are marked by the level of detail: you have zoomed in on the action to tell it with sensory details, great verbs and a big emotional impact. Stories will also need a variety of transitions between scenes and narrative summaries to tie all the parts together. Exposition, or explanations, can come at any point of the story—as long as they don't bog down the story—but often are included in the transitions.

A scene is a contained stretch of action that has a beginning, middle and end. Notice that it is action: characters must do something in a scene, it can't be all internal. Of course, the thoughts are there, too, but the focus of a scene is on the small actions. Somewhere in the scene, there is a pivot point where the actions and emotions spin off in a new direction. It is the fulcrum or balance point for the scene and can come at any point.

Common questions about scenes

1. How long should a scene be? Any length, from a couple lines to a whole chapter. It should be as long as the story needs.

2. Can a scene move from one setting to another? Yes. Movie scripts are written in a slightly different type scene than novels. For scripts, every change of location means a different set up for the camera; so, every setting change—walking from the living room to the front porch—needs a different scene to allow for these camera changes. But for novels, we view a scene as a set of contained actions that relate to a character's goal for those actions. Often, a scene sequence in a movie script would be considered a single scene in a novel.

3. Do scenes have to have one viewpoint character? If you are writing a close, third-person point of view, the scene should stay in that character's point of view throughout the scene. If you are writing omniscient point of view, the scene may encompass several character's points of view.

4. What is scene structure? The structure of a scene is simple: a beginning, a middle and an end. In other words, the actions in a scene must relate to each other and to the central problem or idea presented in that scene. A scene focuses on one central event:

Tell Better Stories for Kids

> *Eli leaves for school*
> *A doctor tells Miriam she has cancer*
> *Felipe climbs a mountain.*

5. How does the scene fit into the overall story? Beyond the basic structure, though, you should know how the scene fits into the overall story, or the function of the scene in the story.

> *When he leaves for school, Eli notices a strange man in the street, a man who will eventually kidnap him—the function of the event is the introduction of the kidnapper.*

Notice that sometimes the event and the function of the event overlap: When Miriam finds out she is dying, it is both the event and the function of the event. But sometimes, the event and its function are slightly different: Eli goes to school; but in the casual mix of his going to school, he gets his first glimpse of the eventual kidnapper.

6. What actions will Show-Don't-Tell this scene? Once you know the central action and how that fits into the story (the function of the scene), you can decide on the actions you will use to Show-Don't-Tell the story at this point. Some writers use a beat sheet, or a listing of the actions. I like to indicate not just the actions, but also the emotions that accompany the actions.

> *Eli runs out front door*
> *Excitement about first day of second grade*
> *Mother calls him back to get his backpack*
> *Embarrassed he forgot, makes him look like a first grader*
> *Eli grabs backpack and runs down steps*
> *Embarrassed that mom is treating him like a first grader*
> *He stops abruptly to tie his shoe and looks back to find Mom watching*
> *Aggravated that it's untied, embarrassment deepens*

> *A strange man almost trips over him*
> *Shiver of fear (This is also the Pivot Point of the scene)*
> *Strange man says something about him being a young man*
> *Pleased that someone notices how grown-up he is*

7. What is the emotional core of this scene? I like listing the emotional responses because it helps me identify the emotional heart of the scene, what Sandra Scofield, author of *The Scene Book*, calls the pulse of a scene. In our example, Eli obviously wants his mom's respect.

Another way to get at this emotional core is to ask, "What is the character fighting for?" Try to make sure the character is fighting for a positive thing—usually someone's love. At the deepest level, characters just want to be loved. Find that positive emotional need somewhere in your story and have your character fight for it.

8. Has something changed in the course of the scene?
By the end of the scene, something must have changed. It may come early and the scene is about dealing with the change, or it may come at the end of the scene. New information comes to light and we suspect it's important information.

> *Someone's feelings/emotions change for the worse.*
> *A character fails to obtain something.*
> *Partial success, but it only brings discouragement; the cup feels half empty, not half full.*
> *Make sure that every single scene has conflict and ends with something worse than before.*

9. Can you improve your scene cuts? In today's fast-paced world, your readers have short attention spans. Often a scene can be deleted, or replaced with a shorter scene. To help identify scenes that might be deleted or cut, ask, "What happened right before this?"

Write out a single sentence that summarizes what happened right before this scene began.

Write a single sentence to summarize this scene.

Does this scene really deserve or need the space that a full scene will take up? Or will a summary work just as well.

For example, when you write a mystery, a character might identify a fingerprint of a suspect. Do you need to show the policemen talking about arresting the suspect? Do you need to show the police locating and arresting the suspect? Maybe you can skip all that and go straight to the interview room with the detective asking the suspect where he was on the night in question. By asking, "What happened right before this?" you may hint at how the suspect tried to run, or how you found him eating a hotdog that dripped ketchup onto his shirt. The scene cut—jumping straight into an interesting scene—though, gives you the economy of effort needed.

10. Where is the humor? Because humor is so valued in a novel, I also try to find a funny spot in the action. Even in the midst of a funeral, people can laugh at a shared memory of the beloved aunt who is gone. Laugher lightens a scene, adds poignancy to tragic circumstances, and best of all, pleases editors and readers.

11. What is the importance of the scene's actions? The scene's actions and its function must be important. If it is too trivial, no one will care; on the other hand, if the event is too large, it can't be contained in a single scene. For example, if a scene centered on whether or not Eli could tie a shoe, it's probably not important enough because there isn't enough at stake emotionally. But Eli can't finish second grade in a single scene, either. A scene has to be a small enough chunk to be contained in a scene, but important enough to need to be covered. This question checks to make sure you've found a balance.

12. What is discovered? Not always, but often, a scene centers around something that is discovered. Perhaps, Eli discovers that his mother is smoking a cigarette. Sometimes, the discovery is something internal: Felipe realizes that the reason he wants to climb the mountain is to prove to his father that he's courageous.

13. Did you use a pivot point? While we can talk about the middle of a scene, it's more helpful to identify a pivot point where the actions and emotions turn to a new direction. For Eli, the pivot point is when the stranger runs into him and he discovers that being grown up might not be safe, that his independence might get him into trouble. For Felipe, the pivot point is when his rope breaks, and he is in danger of falling.

A pivot point might intensify action, turn the emotions in a new direction, or move from humor to emotional connection. It might be an epiphany. The scenes will build up to this point and afterwards, it is a reaction to this point. Each scene needs that pivot point to keep the story's tension high. Without a pivot point, scenes fall flat.

Scenes Worksheet

Choose a scene in your novel and answer these questions in your revision notebook.

SUMMARIZE WHAT HAPPENS IN THIS SCENE, WHAT IS THE MAIN ACTION?

WHAT FUNCTION DOES THIS SCENE HAVE IN THE OVERALL STORY?

LIST THE BEATS AND THE ACCOMPANYING EMOTIONS:

· · ·

BEGINNING

PIVOT

END

WHAT IS HAPPENING EMOTIONALLY? WHAT IS S/HE FIGHTING for? Where or how is s/he searching for love?

WHAT IS THE MOMENT JUST BEFORE?

WHAT IS THE HUMOR?

WHAT IS THE IMPORTANCE?

WHAT IS DISCOVERED?

Scenes Debriefing

After working on scenes, rate your strengths in these areas: 1-strong to 5-weak
    Using action; Show-Don't-Tell. _____
    Scene structure: beginning, middle, end; pivot point. _____
    Emotional core of scenes. _____
    Scene cuts or transitions. _____

Are there any surprises in how well you handled scenes?

List your priorities for revision:

Group Session : Scenes

Scenes are a basic building block of fiction. Consider the novels in your group and discuss any scenes issues as needed: emotional content of scenes, scene cuts, pivot points, conflict, etc.

Plan of Action:

Chapter 4
Plot

The Obligatory Scene

Plot is one of the major places where stories can go wrong. We're going to approach this idea of plotting from a round-about way; and we're going to stay here for a long time. We'll start by looking at your Inventory, at what you wrote about the action of the story and what you wrote about the climax of the story.

While some discuss the biggest scene in the story as a climax, I like the concept of an obligatory scene because it has implications for the entire story. Albert Zuckerman, in *Writing the Blockbuster Novel*, says the obligatory scene is "the scene that must happen or must be made to happen." This is where the story resolves the conflict that was set up. Near the end of the novel, you must provide a emotional scene which brings together the main characters in a life-changing final conflict.

Let's examine this concept of obligatory scenes

1. This conflict is the one to which the entire story has been pointing. The beginning conflict sets up this scene, and you are obliged to include this scene because of what you set up. This means when you revise, you must look at the initial conflict and final resolution and decide if they match up. If they don't, you need to change one or the other.

2. Usually, the obligatory scene includes the major characters. Most often, the protagonist and antagonist meet in a final showdown. Grendel and Beowulf fight. The implication, of course, is that your story actually has both a protagonist (main character) and an antagonist (the opposition, enemy, villain) and that they are actually present in the climax.

3. The obligatory scene should be a big scene, which means that it usually should cover a larger number of pages than other less-important scenes.

4. The obligatory scene is usually one of the most emotionally powerful. It often contains a revelation, a complication, a reversal, a twist, a new meaning for old events, or something else that surprises the reader someway. (These surprises must have been prepared for and be believable.) It is often a cascade of emotional confrontations, taking conflicts between different characters (each with their own subplot) in turn and resolving them.

5. The outcome of the obligatory scene drastically changes the future of an individual character or changes the dynamics between characters. In other words, the outcome has meaning beyond the mere physical actions.

6. Often the setting has a special emotional importance to the main conflict. Or, sometimes, the events occur in a "high" place, such as a rooftop, a cliff, or the mast of a ship, places that symbolize that this is a high point of the story.

7. Another implication is that this scene is actually present in the story. Sometimes writers fear the emotional impact of the scene on

themselves as they write. So the reader is anticipating the big scene and instead turns the page to find that the main character wakes up and deals with the aftermath of the obligatory scene. You must write the scene!

Obligatory Scene Worksheet

In your revision notes, answer these questions.

1. Did you WRITE the obligatory scene, or did you avoid it or skip it or cut it short?
Check one:
I wrote the scene._____
I skipped the scene._____
I wrote the scene, but cut it short._____

DID YOU RESOLVE THE CONFLICT THAT IS SET UP IN THE FIRST chapter/section, or did you resolve a different conflict? If the setup and resolution don't match, which one would you change?

2. WHO IS THE PROTAGONIST? WHO IS THE ANTAGONIST?
Note: The antagonist can be nature or another abstract or inanimate object/ idea. But stories are usually stronger if the novelist finds a way to embody the abstract/inanimate in a person. It's not strictly necessary, and I'm sure you can point to stories which work without this. But in general, novels are stronger when the antagonist is a person. Luke Skywalker faces Darth Vader, not just the abstract evil Empire.

DO THE PROTAGONIST AND ANTAGONIST DIRECTLY (FACE-TO-face) confront each other in the climax?

. . .

What characters are present at the obligatory scene? Who else needs to be present in the climax?

3. Does the obligatory scene have emotional power? Does it have any of these? A revelation, a complication, a reversal, a twist, a new meaning for old events, or something else that surprises the reader someway.

4. Is the conflict between the main characters? Some writers put the sidekick, general, or main character's helper in the scene instead of the main characters themselves. Instead, the main characters must be included. If you have several main characters, you may need a cascade of confrontations between characters: A vs. B, A vs. C, B vs. C. Have you provided appropriate final confrontations for each of these?

5. Does the outcome of the obligatory scene drastically change the future of an individual character or changes the dynamics between characters? How?

6. How many pages does this scene take? Is this considerably more than any other scene in the book?

7. Where does the obligatory scene occur? Is this the most dramatic setting you can imagine for the climax? Where else might it occur that would provide more exciting physical action, more emotional resonance, more dramatic possibilities?

Narrative Arc

If you have the obligatory scene right, then let's back up and look at the rest of your plot.

Plots are a string of incidents that lead to a climax. If you look at the major scenes in your story, you should be able to plot a rising arc of conflict. Story events result in disasters that lead your characters farther and farther away from resolving the conflict.

Too many times, the conflict in a story is resolved too early. Or each chapter resolves its own conflict, leaving no overall conflict to carry the reader forward into the next chapter. We LIKE our characters and we don't want to make things difficult for them!

Gary Schmidt, in the Newbery Honor book, *Lizzie Bright and the Buckminster Boy*, does a great job of ending each scene with a disaster. Study how he tightens the screws on Turner Buckminster, until you think it can't get any worse. And then it does.

Narrative Arc Worksheet

Go back to your Inventory and look at the strongest scenes/chapters in your story: you marked these by circling the chapter numbers. Do these string together to make an arc? The strongest chapter should be the climax. After that, writers vary in their preferences. Some like the opening to be the second strongest chapter; others want to build steadily from the opening to the climax. Consider your story and use your judgment. Regardless of how you actually rank the individual scenes, these strong scenes/chapters should work together to form that narrative arc. Be sure to repeat this for any subplots.

LIST THE PLACES WHERE THE PROTAGONIST AND ANTAGONIST come face to face. Are these the same chapters that you identified as the strongest chapters?

. . .

Does the situation for the main character get worse in each step until the end?

Look at the scenes/chapters you marked as strongest. Is there a gap, a leap, a missing scene?

In the Inventory, you were asked to put a check in the blank if your chapter contained a conflict. Look at any chapters that you did NOT check, that is, that do not have conflict. Probably, you can eliminate these chapters, except for a few details here and there. Or else, you must totally revamp them to include a conflict. Make notes about what you want to do with each of these chapters.

If you did check that conflict is present, look at the end of the chapter. Is the situation worse than at the first of the chapter? In what way? Or, did you resolve the conflict totally? Some up-and-down of events/emotions is OK, but in general, almost all the chapters should end with the situation worse than when it started.

Help for Sagging Middles

Not sure how to make things worse for your characters? Here are some ideas.

Possible Character Actions or Events

- deception
- change in material well-being
- challenge to authority
- guilty conscience/making amends
- conspiracy

search and rescue
mistaken identity
criminal action
suspicion
honor vs. dishonor
Sub-plot that begins and ends within 3-4 chapters in middle of novel: Ex. a riddle or chase.
Other subplots
A different setting—fearful, dreaded
A new fear for a character
Argument about how to approach a problem

Possible Plot Actions or Events

Meeting with a mentor
Make friends.
Make enemies
Go to a watering hole (gathering place in your setting, where discussion can provoke something, or where characters can meet new enemies or allies)
Direct challenge of the character's goal
Indirect challenge of character's goal
Preparation to meet a challenge:
Character learns new skills
Issue a warning
Reorganize a group after a severe test
Overcome emotional resistance within the hero
Crack a joke—comic relief
Death of minor character (Or death of minor character's goal)
Chase scene/action sequence
After a small victory, a time to boast
Time to recommit to goal and face the final challenge
Epiphany—character suddenly understands something
Set a clock ticking—time limit imposed

- Take a side trip that eventually will impact main plot
- Past comes back to haunt character
- Stunning revelation, twist, surprise
- Romantic sub-plot
- Character abandons their goal temporarily
- Shift the balance of power
- Character repents of actions
- Deeper commitments

Microplotting or Pacing

We usually think of plotting as the shape of the overall story. But every section, chapter, scene has events that contribute to plot. The combination of these micro-plotting events adds up to pacing. How closely spaced are these events? How densely packed are they?

In *Making Shapely Fiction,* Jerome Stern talks about Zigzagging, while Albert Zuckerman, in *Writing the Blockbuster Novel,* calls it Story Points. Some writers call these beats.

These are events within a scene that twist the action or develop it in some way on a smaller scale. I describe this as the last two minutes of a basketball game. The red and blue teams are tied: suddenly, the red guard steals the ball and makes a long pass down court to the sprinting forward—who misses the ball; blue takes it out of bounds and has a hard time finding an open man, until the blue guard finally throws it to the breakaway star player, who dribbles hard, stops and shoots a fade-away. Blue leads. Red inbounds, and the red point guard dribbles quickly down court, powers inside and makes an awkward hook shot. The ball rolls around the rim. Will it drop?

The audience's emotions are bouncing around just as much as the basketball. Hurrah! It dropped! Score tied again and blue has a chance to slow down the action—no, the red guard steals the ball and dribbles toward the basket and runs into a blue player. Will the foul be on red for charging or blue for blocking?

Either way, the umpire is in for cat-calls!

That's microplotting.

Microplotting means change in some form: small actions, characters say something, characters learn something, the status of character changes, the dynamics of relationship change, the story raises new questions about the outcome or the consequences, events prepare for and foreshadow later events, and so on.

How do the small actions of a chapter build and develop the main action, leading to the disaster that leaves the character in worse shape at the end of the chapter?

It's easy to think of the main actions of each chapter. It's much harder to zigzag your way through the rest of it with enough significant emotional fluctuations to keep the reader's attention, to keep the scene electric with suspense. But that's your goal.

Microplotting or Pacing Worksheet

Look at one scene in your story, or one chapter and mark the story points (or zigs and zags or beats, whichever terminology you prefer). Gone with the Wind had 24 story points in 21 pages (of typeset text). Based on that standard, you should have at least one story point for each one to two pages of manuscript. How is your story doing?

Exchange that scene with another person in your group and let them mark the story points in the same scene. Do they agree with you about the number of story points? Discuss this to see where you differ in identifying something as a story point.

Plot Debriefing

After working on plot, rate your strengths in these areas:
1-strong to 5-weak

- Narrative Arc_____
- Obligatory scene_____
- Microplotting_____

Are there any surprises in how well you handled plot?

List your priorities for revising plot.

Group Session 2: Plot

Discuss each novel in turn.

> Does the novel set up a conflict for the main character in the first chapter?
> Does the obligatory scene solve that conflict?
> Do the major scenes add up to a rising narrative arc?
> Do chapters end with a worsened situation?

Suggestions/Brainstorming for changes?

Plan of Action:

Chapter 5
Characters

Wooden, lifeless characters are one of the chief opponents of depth. On the Inventory. I asked you to write everything you know about your character from just the first five pages. Typical results are these: name, age, where they live, something about family. That's too generic.

Instead, we need to know things like these: loves licorice; fears granddaddy longlegs; she's in love with Shawillabob Cotton but he doesn't even know her name; he hates it when Mr. Abrams (geometry teacher) leans over his page because of his minty breath; she wants (more than anything else) to run (and win!) the barrel-race in the rodeo next week.

Let's strengthen your characters!

Physical Characteristics

Names

Does a rose by any other name smell as sweet? No.

In *Gone with the Wind*, Scarlett O'Hara would not be the same as if she was named Pansy, as Margaret Mitchell called her in the first draft.

Within a novel, it's confusing if too many character names are similar. On the charts below, mark off when you use a letter to start a first or last name. Try not to repeat any letters:

First Names
A B C D E F G H I J K L M N O P Q R S T U V W X Y Z

Last Names
A B C D E F G H I J K L M N O P Q R S T U V W X Y Z

Think about the connotations of the names. Do you want a name which supports or contrasts with the character's main attributes? Complete this for each main character.

NAME

MAIN CHARACTER QUALITY

SUPPORT / CONTRAST

ALTERNATE NAMES

Character Descriptions

Defy the Cliche: Stories are about people and that means they need strong characterization—the various ways in which you make a character come alive. Often characterizations in first drafts are wooden and cliched. When you revise you must push past these to something more interesting.

> Ex. Mary had blue eyes. (Cliche/wooden)
> Mary's eyes were so blue that the sky looked out of them. (Better—visual)
> Mary wears blue contacts because they transformed her mouse-gray eyes into forceful gaze. (Better—visual, and tells something about character's attitude about herself.)

Push exaggeration, extreme visuals, extreme sensory details, unusual comparisons. Try to make the descriptions do a triple duty: accurate description, full of sensory details, and tells something about the character's attitude.

Exaggeration: Her lipstick was three shades brighter than her age allowed.

Extreme Visual: From across the room, he saw Nancy's ballerina-straight back.

Comparison: When she turned, all he could do was stare at the turquoise maiden. Her eyes were deep-blue, opaque stones regarding him impassively.

For a good example of unique characters, read the young adult novel, *Whale Talk* by Chris Crutcher.

Character Descriptions Worksheet

Defy the Cliches: In your revision notebook, choose a character and decide what attribute you want to work on. At the top of a sheet, write the character's name and attribute. Write words or phrases (don't worry about complete sentences) to describe the person using that attribute. Stretch for the unusual: exaggerate, compare, think "character qualities embodied."

Darcy Pattison

Attributes
Action
Eccentric
Comparison
Face
Body
Arms/legs
Height
Weight
Disposition
Temperament
Uncommon Description
Mannerisms
Transportation
Likes
Dislikes
Cultural bias/prejudices
Clothing

Attitude about _____ (fill in the blank with something appropriate for your story)

WRITE A NEW DESCRIPTION OF YOUR CHARACTERS.

CHARACTER 1:

CHARACTER 2:

CHARACTER 3:

The Emotional Arc and Epiphanies

Look back at the Inventory where you recorded the main emotion of each chapter. Reading through these should give you the emotional arc of your chapter. Like the plot arc, here should be a series of emotional states, changes that result in an emotional climax and a resolution of the emotional conflict. The character is changed in some way.

Often, an epiphany functions as the emotional obligatory scene. Epiphany was originally a religious term for a revelation from God. It was a manifestation: the word becoming flesh. It's commonly used in fiction when the internal life of a character is changed by something that is revealed to them. It's the moment when the character "suddenly realizes."

Placement of an epiphany: An epiphany can function as any of the points on the emotional arc, when it makes the most sense for your character to realize something. Most often, though, epiphanies are associated with the climax of a plot arc and function as the climax of the emotional or internal arc of the story. An epiphany can also trigger the plot climax, come in the middle of the plot climax scene and twist the action a different direction, or come after the plot climax.

Epiphany Mistakes

1. "And then it dawned on her."

The epiphany is cliched and no ground work was laid for it. The revelation is abstract and unemotional. To fix this, approach the revelation indirectly, though imagery, metaphor and symbolism. Build in cause-effect relationships for this new understanding.

2. "In a glorious splash of color and light, the answer—bestowed as if by angels—illuminated all the harsh, cruel suffering of the last horrible year."

The epiphany is expressed in language that is inflated, as if it was an otherworldly religious or spiritual experience. Seldom does this type language work for an epiphany. Instead, keep the language in proportion, using ordinary language and allowing the epiphany to be low-key in the text but resonating in the reader's memory.

3. "See how perceptive and sensitive I am!"

For first-person POV stories, there's a danger of the epiphany sounding self-congratulatory. Be sure to ground the epiphany in concrete details. Or, have the first person narrator report on someone else's epiphany.

4. _____

In effect, the epiphany doesn't exist, because the writer didn't write it. Indirection and implication were taken to the extreme of obscurity. Instead, write the epiphany clearly enough that it is understood, but not so obvious to be blatant. If the character (or the writer) has to explain it, then the epiphany is weak.

5. "He realized that if he turned in his homework and studied for a test, he could make a good grade."

The epiphany is a "Duh!" It's banal, ordinary. Nothing unusual has been revealed, manifested, understood. To cure this type epiphany, think harder! In this epiphany example from my story, ***The Wayfinder***, Win has traveled through the depths of grief over losing his sister, Zanna, and emerged stronger and he's bringing home healing water to his land. But he has to deal with his grief one more time. Paz Naamit is the name of the giant eagle who flies him across the deep canyon. This comes on p. 195 of 200 pages.

> *"Win rose and helped Lady Kala climb onto the broad back of the eagle. When they were both seated, the eagle gave a mighty leap. Her wings spread majestically, and they sailed out over the Rift. Far below, the shiny ribbon of water was still in deep shadow. While his left hand held the water skin upright, Win's right hand crept into his pocket and pulled out the white rock from Zanna's cairn. He had traveled through the depths of the Rift and fought his way to the top and across to the black sand of the Well of Life, then back across the prairie to the Rift again—and Zanna was in none of those places.*
>
> *Instead she was with him and in him. Later, when there was time, he would tell Hazel and Eli his favorite memories of Zanna and listen to theirs. In the telling Zanna would dazzle them once more with her smile. For as long as there were memories or words, Zanna would live. For a moment he hefted the bone white stone in his hand, then reared back and threw it into the Rift, back into the depths from which it had come. It fell soundlessly, and he didn't know when or where it landed. Paz Naamit caught an updraft and spiraled higher and higher. Win laid a hand on Lady Kala's warm back and turned toward G'il Rim and home."*

Here, the imagery of the bone-white stone carries the emotional weight of seeing Zanna's burial place. It is a turning point in Win's grief, the point at which he can no longer deny that she was gone. Throwing the stone back into the Rift, the canyon of grief, means that Win is lighter, that a healing has taken place.

Only at that point can the giant bird "spiral higher and higher" taking Win to that higher spiritual plane.

Connecting the Emotional Arc and Plot Arc

The connection between the inner and outer arcs, the emotional arc and the plot arc isn't always easy to SEE. When you set up an initial plot conflict, you need to immediately ask yourself what obligatory action scene is set up. When the inner conflict is set up, you need to ask what epiphany is set up.

For example: In **The Wayfinder**, the initial conflict is when Win Finds his sister standing on the edge of the Rift and freezes for an instant in fear, thus allowing her to fall to her death. The final conflict again places him on the edge of the Rift (high place with emotional impact) where he faces the same circumstances: someone must fall. How will he react?

In early drafts, I was slightly off bull's-eye in delivering this scene. Win wrestled with his enemy who starts to fall into the Rift, and Win must save her. It worked, but it didn't have quite the emotional impact needed. Instead, I changed the character who falls to Win's new friend. He faces the same circumstances, but this time, he has journeyed far and learned much about himself and he reacts differently. Now, the emotional impact was right on target.

Exercise: The Margins for Emotions

I once got this remark on a rejection for a WIP, an animal fantasy about armadillos entitled, *Vagabonds*: "the characters feel too flat."

"ARGH!" was my heartfelt, emotional response. And since I'd had that comment several times before, I decided to do something about it.

I was thinking of the plot story points and wondering if maybe I had too few emotional zig-zags. I decided to compare the first chapter of *Vagabonds* with a book that was touted for its great characters, *A Great and Terrible Beauty* (Random House) by Libba Bray, abbreviated here as *AGATB*. In the book's margins, I wrote the name of the emotion evoked or mentioned to see if there were many zigzags.

Tell Better Stories for Kids

Analyzing the emotional zig-zags in the first ~100 lines of the two novels. Read down the left-hand column for the beats of *AGATB*, and the right-hand column for *Vagabond*'s beats.

AGATB — VAGABONDS
surprise — pleasure in home
disgust — longing
fear — compulsion to go north
argue with Mom — love of sisters
defiant — special bond with 4th sister
sarcastic — fear
misery at heat — pride
annoyed — relief
thinks of father — wants news
mother sighs — longing
rejected — curious
ignored — rejects request
longing — dismay
stranded — mourning
misunderstood — longing
lonely — coping
annoyed — planning
bored — worry
satisfaction — hope
hope — obedience

While the number of emotional zig-zags are about the same, the depth of emotion in *AGATB* is deeper. Bigger zigs and zags. More and deeper variation. Also, in *Vagabonds*, there are actions that are unaccompanied by emotions, but this never happens in *AGATB*. Even the descriptions carry emotional weight. It's not the amount of emotion, but the quality that sets them apart.

To my surprise, this exercise actually showed me why my story felt flat. I have much more action for my character than *AGATB*, but that's not the key. What matters is using words that carry emotional weight. These words in *AGATB* carry an emotional response to things: hissing, surprisingly, cruel, blue eyes of blindness, good eating.

I was surprised also, that often the emotions were named. Is that Telling, instead of Showing? Ah, it seems that the old adage Show-Don't-Tell doesn't work exactly. It's more like this: Show-and-then-you-can-Tell-emotions-if-you-want.

In these examples, from my WIP novel, I've put in caps the words that carry emotional weight. Of course, it's subjective and another person might mark it differently.

Original Version
Deep under the large oak, Galen, the nine-banded armadillo YAWNED. It was a RARE moment: the Four Sisters all slept at the same time. He tiptoed around them, pausing to tuck a bit of moss around Number Three's toes, and reached the den entrance without waking anyone.

Revised Version
Deep under the large oak, Galen, the nine-banded armadillo yawned in FATIGUE. It was a RARE moment: the Four Sisters all slept at the same time. Stifling another yawn, he tiptoed around them, trying to STEAL a bit of privacy. He paused to AFFECTIONATELY tuck a bit of moss around Number Three's toes: she was always cold. To his SURPRISE, he reached the den entrance without waking anyone.

Not, perhaps, the best, but there's more emotional weight. If I carry this out throughout the story, then maybe the characters won't feel so flat. In the first version, I did a good job of using active verbs, strong images, etc. But I didn't interpret everything through my main character's eyes. No wonder it leaves readers cold and seems flat!

Evaluate the Emotions in Your Story

In the margins of your mss, write the emotions evoked for the first 100 lines, or about four to five pages. What do you observe about the emotional weight of your story? Highlight the words that carry emotion. Are they unusual and striking? Would a different word evoke better emotion?

Emotional Arc and Epiphany Worksheet

Go back to your Inventory and look at the strongest scenes/chapters in your story: you marked these by circling the chapter numbers. Are these also the chapters with the strongest emotions? If not, decide on the strongest emotions of the story and mark them. Do these strong emotions string together to make an arc?

Often, the first and last acts of a novel are setup and resolution of the external plot. That leaves the middle, or the second act, for the most development of the inner arc. If you find that most of the emotional arc occurs during the second act, that's fine; if it's spread out across all three acts, that's fine, too. Evaluate your story:

IS THERE A GAP, A LEAP, A MISSING EMOTIONAL SCENE?

DOES YOUR CHARACTER HAVE AN EPIPHANY?
___Yes___No___More than one.

HOW DOES THE EPIPHANY RELATE TO THE EMOTIONAL resolution? Can you tighten that relationship?

. . .

How does the character change emotionally over the course of the novel?

Did you Show or Tell the epiphany? If you told, how can you show?

How can you set up the epiphany so it is earned and convincing?

Does the climax of the emotional arc occur during or near the Obligatory Scene? What changes could make the relationship between the obligatory scenes for plot and emotions hit a bull's eye?

Repeat this exercise for any subplots.

Raising the Stakes

How do you make the story matter more? Examples include giving characters unusual motives, giving the person a high personal worth, raising the stakes, putting more at risk, forcing a person to violate a moral code, the character willingly makes a sacrifice.

Opposite Motives

Pick one scene where the characters take an unusual action:
What is the character's motive for this action?

. . .

WHAT IS THE OPPOSITE OF THAT MOTIVE?

HOW WOULD THE SCENE BE DIFFERENT IF THE OPPOSITE MOTIVE was the real motive? How could you make that work? Repeat for several scenes throughout the story.

Put More at Stake

As your character works toward his/her goal, what is at stake? If s/he doesn't succeed—so, what?

TRY TO RAISE THE STAKES BY DOING ONE OR BOTH OF THESE:
    1. Put more at risk. What else could be at stake? So what? What would make this matter even more?
    2. Force character to choose if s/he will violate a moral code. What moral codes do they hold? How could you challenge them?

SO WHAT? WHAT WOULD CHALLENGE THEIR MORAL CODE IN A more emotional way?

COULD THIS MORAL CODE BE THE REASON WHY A CHARACTER willingly makes a sacrifice?

Villains

Characters gain personal worth when others like them. Even villains have pets who like them.

Develop Your Villain

Villain (antagonist): Who likes the villain? Who thinks the villain has great personal worth. Why? Can you add backstory to explain why this/these character(s) likes the villain?

Look for a place where you dislike the villain the most. At that point, how can you work in a tender scene with the villain's friend. Repeat for other main characters, as needed.

Dialogue

In his book, *Writing Dialogue*, Tom Chiarella says, "Your challenge is to see the stories within the words of your character." Listen to this mother getting her daughter out of bed on a school morning:

> *I don't have time to be gentle.*
> *Eyes open? That helps.*
> *No, you can't consistently count on it. It's not your car.*

Just from three lines from one character, you can see the conflict brewing on this morning, just as surely as the coffee is brewing. You don't even need the daughter's responses. From these three lines, here are some things we know:

- The mother is in a hurry and isn't sympathetic to the daughter's wish to sleep longer.
- Possibly, the mother isn't a morning person; we'll hold off on that assumption until we have more evidence.
- Daughter is definitely not a morning person.
- Daughter is probably about 16 or 17 years old since she's driving, but doesn't own a car yet.
- Mother doesn't much like sharing a car with Daughter.

In just three lines of dialogue, we have characterization, action that advances the story, emotional impact and micro-conflicts. That's what you want your dialogue to do for your story.

SKIT: Football Star or Drug Junkie?

To jump start a dialogue that isn't working try giving the characters attitudes that are in opposition. With a group, try this improvisational dialogue. Ask for two volunteers and give each one set of the instructions here; make sure neither knows the others' instructions.

1. You are the Principal of a school. You have called Mrs. Jones in, because you found her son smoking marijuana in the bathroom. By the way, you stutter and you stutter even worse when you're under stress.

2. You are Mrs. Jones. Your son is the football team's star quarterback. At least you think so. But he only got five minutes playing time last week. This week, college scouts will be at the game. You are determined to convince the Principal that your son should start on offense. You never take "No" for an answer.

What do you observe about the interaction between the principal and mother? Is there conflict? Who has the most at stake? Is the dialogue always in complete sentences?

Note: If you're doing this book on your own, write out the dialogue that might ensue. By giving each character a certain attitude, and a single character quality, the dialogue is set up to be dynamic.

Dialogue Techniques

Dialogue is often written as an exchange between two characters, with each character getting their say in turn. But you have options:

Interruption.
Son: Can I drive to the—
Mom: Did you get your room cleaned up?

Silences.
Son: Can I drive to the football game tonight?
Mom:
Son: Did you hear me? Can I drive?

Echoes (or near echo).
Son: Can I drive to the football game tonight?
Mom: You want to go to the football game?

Reversals.
Son: Can I drive to the football game tonight?
Mom: You can take the mini-van.
Son: You know what? I don't want to go.

Shifts in tone and pace.
Son: Can I drive to the football game tonight?
Mom: Let's see. If we have hot wings and a baked potato for supper, will that work?

Idioms or jargon.
Son: Kick-off is at 7:30. Can I drive the F-150?
Mom: Cheers have to be there early. Can you take your sister?

Answer a question with a question.
Son: Can I drive to the football game tonight?
Mom: How'd you do on the algebra test?

Don't answer a question.
Son: Can I drive to the football game tonight?
Mom: It's time for supper. Wash up.

Talk to someone offstage.
Son: Can I drive to the football game tonight?
Mom, into cell phone: Did you decide? A movie or not?

Answering questions with answers that aren't quite answers but sound like them.
Son: Can I drive to the football game tonight?
Mom: You did get an A in your driver's ed class.

Allowing characters to speak to themselves, for themselves.
Son: Can I drive to the football game tonight?
Mom: He wants to go to the game. But did he clean his room? Did he even put his dirty towels in the laundry this morning?

Carrying on more than one conversation at a time.
Son: Can I drive to the football game tonight?
Daughter: I want to go to the 7:30 movie.
Mom: What time?
Son: Don't make me take her.
Daughter: 7:30. I told you.
Mom: The game. What time does the game start?

Details.
Son: Can I drive the convertible to the 7:30 football game tonight? I want to pick up Melissa at 7 and take a spin through the park.
Mom: No. Melissa smokes. She goes nowhere in my car.

Use dialogue as an entry point for a flashback.
Son: Can I drive to the football game tonight?
Mom remembers the last football game of her high school years, the one where she was head cheerleader and met Joe, the captain of the opposing football team, the man she finally married.

Dialogue Mechanics

For dialogue tags, I seldom use anything besides "said." The actual words of the character should already reflect tone, emotion, attitude. Also, avoid adverbs and present participles:

Added Adverbs: "she said quaintly."
Added Present Participle: "he said, scratching his nose."

These work occasionally, but either can become a distinct habit. Eliminate all dialogue tags, except s/he said, until the habit's broken. Instead, omit the action or use a separate sentence with the action more direct or more interesting.

Dialogue worksheet

Most dialogue is too long winded, too formal, and includes too much information. Sometimes, it's helpful to isolate the dialogue and work on it without the scene or actions interfering.

Choose a piece of dialogue that isn't working, about 10-20 lines of exchange. Cut out all scenic detail and actions of characters, leaving just the dialogue. For example, in a novel I'm working on, two characters are trying to decide if they will move forward or head back home. V is hoping that success will mean a ballad is sung in their honor. G plays on his vanity to convince him to go forward.

G: You're thinking too small.
V: I think small?
G: Compare ballads: finding trekkers or finding the Falls.
V: You'd risk everything?
G: Wouldn't you?
V: Rafael's blind. He can't travel.
G: Think of it: the Ballad of the Faralone Falls.
V: El Garro needs to know.
G: Why?
V: Because he needs to know.
G: Rafael sings the Turi's song.

V: You would risk everything? For that song?
G: No. For my sisters. For our people.
V: (Silence)
G: They are the reason to risk everything.
V: The Ballad? The reason...
G: ...to risk everything.

Once I was satisfied, I spread out this dialogue over the course of an entire chapter full of travel and action, which helped it seem like the decision took a long time. For another great example of succinct dialogue see the last few lines of Chapter 1 of *Samurai Shortshop* by Alan Gratz.

Re-Write Your Dialogue

To get started:

> Decide what each character wants.
> Give each character an attitude.
> Avoid exposition—characters talk to each other, not to the reader.
> Do not explain things that the characters would already know.
> Cut to the bare bones, making each piece of dialogue really count.
> Read aloud for rhythms.
> Use some of the techniques explained earlier of interruption, silences, echoes,
> reversals, shifts in tone and pace, idioms, etc.

In your revision notebook, work on dialogue techniques. The space is deliberately small, just one line for each piece of dialogue, to encourage you to keep it bare bones.

A:
B:
A:
B:
A:
B:
A:
B:
A:
B:
A:
B:
A:
B:
A:
B:
A:
B:
A:
B:
A:
B:
A:
B:
A:
B:
A:
B:

To judge the effectiveness of dialogue, use this checklist:

_____The purpose of the exchange is clear.

_____The dialogue captures the reader's interest.

_____The dialogue creates tension.

_____The exchange builds to a micro-climax.

_____Regardless of what was said, the aftermath creates some change: emotions soar or dip, information is exchanged, relationships change somehow, the plot heads in a new direction, etc.

If you are satisfied with the resulting dialogue, insert it back into the text and read through, adjusting details as needed.

Opening with Character

By now, you've worked on the characters' names, descriptions, epiphanies, emotional arcs, stakes, and dialogue. What's left? Look back at the Inventory. You were asked to read only the first five pages of your novel and write down everything you know about your character. Often, I find that the list reads something like this:

John—teenager
His parents are mad at him because he's lazy
John has a dog (but I don't know what kind)

Instead, look at this list of characteristics from the first five pages of *Lizzie Bright and the Buckminster Boy* by Gary Schmidt:

Name: Turner Buckminster
Just moved to Phippsburg Maine, where his father will be minister
Likes the sea
Hates Phippsburg after just six hours
Doesn't like being a minister's son—he worries about what folks think
The Phippsburg welcome for the pastor's family was warm
The Phippsburg children's welcome for the new minister's son was cool
Turner wants to belong

Turner loves to play baseball—Boston style, not Phippsburg style—and is confident of his abilities until he sees the Phippsburg style of pitching
Nice rapport with Mom

The beginnings of Turner's internal and external conflicts play out against the scene of the strange way of playing baseball. By the end of the game/scene, Turner is already turning against Phippsburg society's way of doing things.

Your Character's Beginning

Now that you've done other exercises to strengthen your character, does your opening reveal enough about your main character? How could you you begin your story to let his/her characteristics start to shine? Write a new opening, focusing on letting the main character take center stage and revealing enough character to intrigue the reader.

Characters Debriefing

After working on characters, rate your strengths in these areas:
    1-strong to 5-weak

  Character names_____
  Character descriptions_____
  Raising the Stakes_____
  Dialogue_____
  Character in Opening Pages_____

ARE THERE ANY SURPRISES IN HOW WELL YOU HANDLED CHARACTER?

. . .

Tell Better Stories for Kids

LIST YOUR PRIORITIES FOR REVISION.

Group Session 3: Characters

Discuss the characterization of each novel in your group.
   Think about the differences in these:

prehistory—the general background of a place and time
biography—personal histories that add depth to characters
backstory—specific actions which set-up the story's conflict.

Some suggest that you leave backstory out until at least halfway through a novel; others recommend putting backstory in chapter two. Almost everyone agrees that chapter one should have absolutely no backstory, opting instead for a powerful scene that draws the reader into the characters' current lives. Personally, I try to push it as late as possible.
   Discuss each novel in terms of prehistory, biography and backstory. What should you include/exclude from each, especially in the beginning chapters?
   Alternate discussion topic: Select a section of dialogue and assign roles. Read the section aloud and listen to the speech patterns of each character. Are they distinct? Does the dialogue move the story forward? Would it benefit from judicious cutting?

PLAN OF ACTION:

Chapter 6
Choosing Details

Human beings understand the world around them through their senses. Likewise, clear writing gives specific details that makes the reader experience the story/idea better.

We'll jump right in with an exercise to find the sensory details used in a piece of writing. In the excerpt on the following page, mark each sense with a different color. There may be some overlap—if there is mark it with both colors.

Visual details (things you see)—red, or underline
Olfactory details (things you smell)—blue, or square
Gustatory details (things you taste)—Green, or circle
Auditory details (things you hear)—yellow, or squiggly line underneath
Kinesthetic (how it feels to move in space)
Tactile details (Things you feel: temperature, texture)—purple, or parentheses

Darcy Pattison

THE STRANGE BUG

Jessie Ford pushed pink cotton balls between her toes, then shook the bottle of "Peach" nail polish, the new color for summer. On the dressing table sparkled forty-six other colors of polish. In the middle of the first year of culinary school, she'd suddenly rebelled at the stark white chef uniforms. She started using toe polish for a splash of color and somehow found time to change the color every day. The familiar acetone smell woke her up better than the bitter taste of coffee.

Bzzz! Bzzz!

Jessie pivoted, searching anxiously for the wasp. It was on the balcony window, just like the others had been. She slid open the glass doors, which were already warm from the summer sunshine. Maybe the wasp would fly out. Careful of the cotton balls squishing between her toes, Jessie thumped on her heels to the kitchen and grabbed the fly swat and bug spray. She thumped back to her bedroom, almost slipping on the shiny wooden floor. Just holding the can of bug spray, it smelled disgusting. The glossy black wasp had flown out! It alighted on the balcony railing and quivered in the warm breeze. Jessie caught sight of her reflection in the balcony window. She was balanced on her heels, with a fly swat raised in her right hand and a can of bug spray in her left hand. She still wore the frayed cotton robe and her damp hair was wrapped in a towel. Suddenly, she laughed. She looked like a strange bug, too.

With a clank, Jessie slid the balcony door closed. She dropped the fly swat and bug spray on the dresser and picked up the Peach nail polish again.

Evaluating Sensory Details

There are physical or kinesthetic details: pushed, shook, pivoted, slid, thump, slipping, squishy cotton balls, balanced, dropped (Notice that lots of the kinesthetic details will be great action verbs.)

There are visual details: pink cotton balls, sparkling colors of nail polish, stark white uniform, glossy black wasp, shiny wooden floor, quivering, frayed cotton robe, wrapped in towel, looked like a strange bug (Notice that similes and metaphors will often go here.)

There are auditory details: Bzzz!, slip open doors, thump, laugh, clank

There are tactile details: cotton balls, warm glass, warm breeze

There are olfactory details: acetone, coffee, bug spray

There are taste details: bitter coffee

These sensory details make sure that the writer follows the advice given to every beginning writer: SHOW, DON'T TELL. Good fiction and even some non-fiction dramatizes action, rather than just tells the action.

Compare this version with the original:

Jessie was painting her toe nails when she heard a bug. She opened the balcony door, hoping it would fly away. She ran to the kitchen for the fly swat and bug spray. She hated bugs. The bug was outside on the balcony! She caught sight of herself in the mirror and decided she looked like a bug, too. With a laugh, she closed the balcony door and went back to painting her toe nails.

The same information is given in both accounts, but the original version gives specific sensory details. It Shows, instead of Tells. This may seem like a simple thing to do—and it is. But it has the potential to make the most amount of difference in your writing.

Sensory Details Exercise

I consider this The Basic Exercise for any fiction writer, the ability to bring a scene to life with well-chosen details. When I'm stuck and don't know where to start the next chapter, this is the exercise that carries me through the process.

Darcy Pattison

Directions for Sensory Details Exercise

Choose a scene from your novel and glance at it briefly to refresh your memory about what happens. Then put the manuscript away; don't refer to it again until you finish this exercise.

Think about the scene. Where does it take place? Close your eyes and pretend you are there, experiencing everything that your main character experiences. What do you see? Hear? Feel? Smell? Touch? Taste?

On a page of your revision notebook, jot down exact words or phrases that describe these details; don't worry about writing complete sentences. Consider this as deposits in a Word Bank: you are putting strong words and images into a word bank and can withdraw them as needed as you write.

Try to write at least three specific details for each sense. Depending on your scene, some senses may be harder than others. For example, taste is easy at a banquet, but harder in the middle of a cave. But push hard to get as many details on each sense as possible, preferably at least three for each sense.

Also, remember to be specific. Not "dog," but "standard poodle that limps."

The other variable here is your particular style of perception. Some people are visual, while others key into sounds. Watch to see which sense is easy or hard for you. When you identify your bent, then work to become stronger in details for other senses.

After you have at least three specific details for each sense, rewrite your story using some of those details. As you write other details may occur to you. That's fine. Use them if you want. Write until you feel you've put in every detail you can. Later you can go back and take some out, but for now concentrate on adding as many sensory details as possible.

Remember: Strong writing tends to ground a scene with at least three types of sensory details. Weak writing only includes visual details.

Sensory Details Worksheet

See

Hear

Feel

Smell

Taste

• • • • • • •

Sensory Details Debriefing

After working on adding effective details, rate your strengths in these areas:
 1-strong to 5-weak

 Using effective sensory details_____
 Are there any surprises in how well you handled sensory details?

List your priorities for revising:

Group Session 4: Sensory Details

Mark a place in your manuscript where you used good sensory details and another place where you need work. Share these sections with your group and discuss.

Plan of Action:

Chapter 7
Language

Good writing uses strong vocabulary. We'll take a quick look at some basics of strong vocabulary and then move quickly to a more advanced discussion. Good communication through the written medium takes an image or idea in my mind and, through words, recreates that image or idea exactly in the reader's mind. One goal then is exact communication.

Verbs

Consider these two sentences:

> Mary walked through the streets.
> Mary shoved through the streets.

Which gives a better image? The second sentence substitutes a more specific verb for the generic "walked" resulting in better communication of the exact situation that Mary faces. And all we did was substitute one word. What if we added a modifier to "walked"?

Mary walked forcefully through the streets.

The image is still not as sharp as it is with the stronger verb, "shoved." A specific verb conveys a picture much better than a weak verb with modifiers. Whenever possible, substitute a strong verb for an verb, plus modifier.

Avoid to-be verbs whenever possible.

To-be verbs (is, are, has, had, am, was, etc.) which tell the state-of-being can also be weak. Consider the following:

The sun is shining on the water.
Sunlight sparkled off the water

Certainly, the to-be verbs are workhorses and do much of the work in sentences; but it's easy to overuse to-be verbs. Whenever possible, omit these verbs and instead substitute a stronger action verb.

Likewise, avoid adverbs when possible. Instead, use a stronger verb.

The sunlight shone brightly off the water.
The sunlight sparkled off the water.

Power up your Nouns

Likewise, strong nouns strengthen writing. If I say the word "Fish," do you have a good image of what that looks like? Well, there are billions and billions of fish in the world in all sizes, shapes and colors.

If I say the word, "Catfish," do you have a good image of what that looks like? Better. Now, there are only millions and millions of catfish from which to choose.

Does this description communicate better? "A catfish with five hooks in his mouth, hooks left-over from the five times he was almost caught but got away." That wily, old catfish can't be confused with any other catfish in the world!

For strong writing, then, use the most specific noun possible; only after you have the most specific noun possible can you add modifiers. Of course, a rule like this is too arbitrary. There are times when it's best to write "a big fish." But do it intentionally, because it's best for a young audience, or it's the most appropriate wording for this story.

Revise for Stronger Words

Find a section of your writing that you suspect is weaker than other sections. Go through the section, trying to choose better words.

Verbs. Especially concentrate on omitting adverbs and other modifiers and substituting action verbs for to-be verbs. Modifiers should be added only after you have the most specific verb possible.

Nouns. Where can you replace a generic noun with a specific noun? Where can you omit modifiers in favor of a more specific noun? If you already have a specific noun, will modifiers help the communication be more exact?

Word Connotations

Mark Twain has said, "The difference between the right word and the nearly right word is the same as that between lightning and lightning bug."

A professional writer must be a lover of words: it is the basis of their craft. The following was written by Bill Marsteller, president of an advertising company, talking about how words can be used to communicate advertising messages. But it does much more than that: it is a rare demonstration of the power of connotation.

Darcy Pattison

The Wonderful World of Words
by Bill Marsteller

HUMAN BEINGS COME IN ALL SIZES, A VARIETY OF COLOR, IN different ages, and with unique, complex and changing personalities.

So do words.

There are tall, skinny words, and short, fat ones, and strong ones and weak ones, and boy words and girl words.

For instance, title, lattice, latitude, lily, tattle, Illinois, and intellect are all lean and lanky. While these words get their height partly out of t's and l's and I's, other words are tall and skinny without a lot of ascenders and descenders. Take, for example, Abraham, peninsula and ellipsis, all tall.

Here are some nice short-fat words: hog, yogurt, bomb, pot, bon-bon, acne, plump, sop and slobber.

Sometimes a word gets its size from what it means but, of course, sometimes it's just how the word sounds. Acne is a short-fat word even though pimple, with which it is associated, is a puny word.

There's a difference between tall-skinny words and puny words. Totter is out-and-out puny, while teeter is more than just slender. Tea, tepid, stool and wary are puny.

Puny words are not the same as feminine words. Feminine words are such as tissue, slipper, cute, squeamish, peek, flutter, gauze and cumulus. Masculine words are like bourbon, rupture, oak, cartel, steak and socks. Words can mean the same thing and be of the opposite sex. Naked is masculine, but nude is feminine.

Just as feminine words are not necessarily puny words, masculine words are not necessarily muscular. Muscular words are thrust, earth, girder, ingot, cask, Leo, ale, bulldozer, sledge and thug. Fullback is very muscular; quarterback is masculine but not especially muscular.

Words Have Colors, Too

Red: fire, passion, rape, explode, smash, murder, lightning, attack.

Green: moss, brook, cool, comfort, meander, solitude, hammock.

Black: glower, agitate, funeral, dictator, anarchy, thunder, tomb, somber, cloak.

Beige: unctuous, abstruse, surrender, clerk, conform, observe, float.

San Francisco is a red city; Cleveland is beige, Asheville is green and Buffalo is black.

Shout is red, persuade is green, rave is black and listen is beige.

One of the More Useful Characteristics of Words is Their Age

There's youth in go, pancake, hamburger, bat, ball, frog, air, surprise, morning and tickle. Middle age brings moderate, agree, shade, stroll and uncertain. Fragile, lavender, astringent, fern, velvet, lace, worn and Packard are old. There never was a young Packard, not even the touring car.

Mostly, religion is old. Prayer, vespers, choir, Joshua, Judges, Ruth and cathedral are all old. Once, temple was older than cathedral and still is in some parts of the world, but in the United States, temple is now fairly young. Saturday, the seventh day of the week, is young, while Sunday the first day of the week, is old. Night is old, and so, although more old people die in the hours of the morning just before dawn, we call that part of the morning, incorrectly, night.

Some words are worried and some radiate disgusting self-confidence. Pill, ulcer, twitch, itch, stomach and peek are all worried words. Confident, smug words are like proud, major, divine, stare, dare, ignore, demand. Joe is confident; Horace is worried.

Now about Shapes

For round products, round companies or round ideas use dot, bob, melon, loquacious, hock, bubble and bald. Square words are, for instance, box, cramp, sunk, block, and even ankle. Ohio is round, but

Iowa, a similar word, is square but not as square as Nebraska. The roundest city is, of course, Oslo. Some words are clearly oblong. Obscure is oblong (it is also beige) and so are platter and meditation (which is also middle-aged). The most oblong lake is Ontario, even more than Michigan, which is also surprisingly muscular for an oblong, though not nearly as strong as Huron, which is more stocky. Lake Pontchartrain is almost a straight line. Lake Como is round and very short and fat. Lake Erie is worried.

Some words are shaped like Rorschach ink blots. Like drool, plot, mediocre, involvement, liquid, amoeba and phlegm. At first blush (which is young), fast words seem to come from a common stem (which is puny). For example, dash, flash, bash and brash are all fast words. However, ash, hash and gnash are all slow. Flush is changing. It used to be slow, somewhat like sluice, but it is getting faster. Both are wet words, as is Flushing, which is really quite dry compared to New Canaan, which sounds drier but is much wetter. Wilkinsburg, as you would expect, is dry, square, old and light gray.

But back to motion.

Raid, rocket, piccolo, hound, bee and rob are fast words. Guard, drizzle, lard, cow, sloth, much and damp are slow words. Fast words are often young and slow words old, but not always. Hamburger is young and slow, especially when uncooked. Astringent is old but fast. Black is old, and yellow—almost opposite on the spectrum—is young, but orange and brown are nearly next to each other and orange is just as young as yellow while brown is only middle-aged. Further, purple, though darker than lavender, is not as old; however, it is much slower than violet, which is extremely fast.

Lavender is actually a rather hard word. Not as hard as rock, edge, point, corner, jaw, trooper, frigid or trumpet, but hard nevertheless. Lamb, lip, thud, sofa, fuzz, stuff, froth and madam are soft. Although they are the same thing, timpani are harder than kettle drums, partly because drum is a soft word (it is also fat and slow), and as pots and pans go, kettle is one of the softer.

There is a Point to all This

Ours is the business of imagination. We are employed to make corporations personable, to make useful products desirable, to clarify ideas, to create friendships in the mass for our employers.

We have great power to do these things. We have power through art and photography and graphics and typography and all the visual elements that are part of the finished advertisement.

And these are great powers. Often it is true that one picture is worth ten thousand words.

But not necessarily worth one word. If it's the right word.

Connotations Speaking to Connotations

John Ciardi and Miller Williams, in *How Does a Poem Mean?*, talk about connotations speaking to connotations. If a story is a context for making choices, then part of the word choices is connotations.

Example: fire, inferno, blaze. These all mean roughly the same thing, but within the context of a story, one may make more sense than another. What are some of the factors that determine which is best?

1. Word Derivations. Fire comes from the Old English (before 900), fyr. Inferno comes Italian/Latin (1825-35) meaning hell and implies a furnace or oven. Blaze comes from Old English (before 1000) meaning a torch or flame.

Do you want a Latin based word or the Anglo-Saxon based words? Which derivation comes closer to what you want?

2. Syllables. Fire and blaze only have one syllable. Inferno has three. Which better fits the rhythm of the voice you've set up?

3. Sound. Fire begins with a harsh sound, but tapers off with the liquid r sound. Blaze has strong sounds at the beginning (bl) and ending (z). Inferno is smoother at the beginning and end, but has the harsher f sound in the middle.

The connotations of a word depend on all these things, plus any cultural or personal associations a person has for the word. For example, depending on the needs of your story, inferno seems to go on and on, while fire seems more finite.

Marsteller's essay shows that words pick up connotations from the way it looks, sounds, derivations, culture, experiences, and more. He talks about words in terms of gender, age, strength, color. It can be confusing to think about words in terms of height and speed, for example. But this is connotation at work within a story.

Connotation Worksheet

As an exercise in connotation, choose a topic, for example, presidents, types of jewelry, countries, book titles, or farm animals. Then, choose several categories of things that could be used to describe the first list, thinking about the connotations of the descriptive words.

For example, the first category might be actresses: Halle Berry, Julia Roberts, Judy Dench. The description categories might be cookies, trees and cars. If you think about the connotations, what kind of cookie describes each actress?

Remember that you are thinking about connotations (gender, age, strength, color, shape, speed, how the words sound, how the words look, how many syllables are in each word, etc.). Try not to think of associations that come from real life: for example, don't describe Hilary Clinton as a Chocolate Chip cookie.

Depending on your experience, this might seem a profound or a silly exercise. But it's one that points the direction toward thinking about words more carefully, based on their connotations.

Connotations Examples

Actress : Halle Berry
Cookie: Chocolate Chip
Tree: Live Oak
Car: Mustang

Actress: Julia Roberts
Cookie: Oatmeal
Tree: Willow
Car: Hummer

Actress: Judi Dench
Cookie: Shortbread
Tree: English Walnut
Car: BMW

Choose your own categories and fill in connotation words. This is also a fun group activity.

Your Connotations

Within your story, what connotations will speak to other connotations? For example, Your story might have repeated mentions of fire, fountains, and football games. Will any of these help you make word choices within the context of your story?

Example: Fire

Competition—fire in the gut, his calf muscles burned with the efforts of the sprint

Romance—fire in their hearts, a volcano of emotions erupted when he saw her

Anger—fire in his eyes; his resentment lay smoldering, like a banked fire, waiting for the right moment to blaze up again

Or, if you have a story about a mother's smothering emotions, which would she serve for dinner: chicken fried steak or liver smothered in onions? What connotations of words, details, or even choice of events would support the emotions of your story?

Choose a section of your novel. Thinking about connotations, evaluate your your word choices. Are there places to revise?

Word Banks

Just as you might research facts, I also research vocabulary and language to use in a story. I create Word Banks, or word lists, from which I can withdraw the currency of golden words when needed. I seldom use everything I deposit into a Word Bank, but it's comforting to know that there is still something in savings.

Word Bank Options

1. Sensory Detail Word Bank, as discussed in the previous section.

2. Historical Word Bank. For historical fiction, I collect words, jargon, slang, details, etc. from that time period.

3. Cultural Word Bank. For my picture book, *The River Dragon*, I researched Chinese language, culture, clothing, etc. I looked especially for descriptive phrases that clearly evoked the culture, without having to stop and say it. For example, I found these descriptions of women: peach-perfect mouth, jade-fine fingers. I used the jade-fine fingers in the story, and I'm saving peach-perfect mouth for another time.

4. Contemporary Word Bank. Jargon and slang come and go so quickly that few try to put the latest slang into a story for fear it will become dated too quickly. The same for clothing styles. Still, there are things that you can look for in contemporary settings. For example, you might talk about computers or cell phones in your story. Again, you wouldn't want to talk abut specific models of phones, but the more generic terminology.

5. General Language Word Bank. Do you ever hear phrases that evoke such a great image that you want to remember them? This is the place for fun phrases, sonorous phrases, melodic phrases, mellifluous phrases, wonderful phrases, or any other language play that fits your current story.

This is the place to play around and find the best way to say things.

Language Debriefing

After working on words, rate your strengths in these areas: 1-strong to 5-weak

Using strong verbs____
Using specific nouns_____
Using word connotations_____
Are there any surprises in how well you handled words?

List your priorities for revision:

Group Session 5: Language

We just scratched the surface of what you might consider in evaluating the language of a story. Consider the novels in your group and discuss any language issues as needed: word choices, sentence structure, sentence variety, sentence length, clarity, cohesion, etc.

Plan of Action:

Chapter 8
Setting

Setting Reinforces Theme

A strong sense of place can be very important to a story. Descriptions need to be interwoven with the thoughts and actions of a character. The way the setting affects the character is what is critical.

> Damon slowly turned in a circle studying the line where the horizontal yellow stretched out to meet the horizontal blue. He was the center of a platter that spun round and round without a wobble, without a break, without a hesitation. The sky wasn't a bowl above him but was a flat plane that somehow—without curving—met the flat yellow land. Alone. Not even a bird in the sky.
>
> Then, Dad was walking toward him. He loomed large, an immense dark slash against the yellow and blue, breaking the horizon with his verticality.

Even before I tell you, can you guess that Dad is about to leave

Damon? The landscape speaks of loneliness before Dad ever opens his mouth.

In one story that I've written, the setting was the key in knowing how to write it. I wanted to write a story about chili. When I decided to set it long the Santa Fe Trail, then the rest of the story fell into place.

Do any of your favorite novels have a strong sense of place? Is the setting important to the outcome of the story? What happens to that story if you change the setting? If the setting is a school, how would that setting differ in Hawaii, Alaska, Texas, Florida, New Hampshire? Don't use a generic setting!

Setting Through the Character's Eye: Mood

Setting is one of the best ways to affect the mood of the story. Mood is the emotional feel of a story, such as scary, sad, optimistic, judgmental. Here is where the author's skill in selection becomes evident, as s/he selects the right details from among the myriad of details possible. Just because a bee is buzzing around a flower, doesn't mean you want to use that sound in your story. Or, the way in which you describe that insect's noise (e.g. angry buzzing, placid droning, Bzzz, Bzzzt) may influence the mood.

Creating Mood Through Details

Here's a description of a tree outside a man's house.

> The tall oak stood beside his house. He passed it every day when he walked out to get in his car. The ground crunched with dead leaves. Looking up, he saw a bird's nest in the top branches.

Here's the same tree in the winter from the viewpoint of a man on his way to the hospital to see his wife who has cancer:

Tell Better Stories for Kids

Nestled in the crook of the top most branches, the nest swayed. A feather fluttered out, caught in the wind and spun upward. It stuck on a bare branch, hesitated, then the wind caught it again. This time it floated down through the naked branches. Down. Rough bark caught at it, but it kept falling anyway. It landed at his feet. He knelt and picked it up. It was a Blue Jay feather, as blue as Amelia's eyes. He craned his neck toward the nest and wished somehow that he could put the feather back where it belonged.

Do you feel the difference in moods between the two pieces? They were created by a careful selection of words and sensory details.

When creating a story's mood, writers have two choices. First, you can choose to reinforce the mood, as above. The man feels that his emotions are bare and exposed to rough winds and that Amelia is somehow moving away from him; these feelings are echoed in the winter tree, with the deteriorating bird nest. Or, you can choose to contrast with the mood of what is happening. When characters fight, it's one of the prettiest days of spring. Here's an example of a tragic situation, made more poignant as it is counterpointed with an odd situation.

My grandmother was in the hospital, dying from old age: she was 99 years old. Her thin white hair wisped around her face, giving her a wrinkled-pixie-look, a pixie who was lost in the white pillow. Hundreds of orange-and-black lady bugs crawled all over the wall, in the florescent light above her bed, around her face on the pillow. They seemed to respect her, staying around her, but never crawling on her, as if even their fragile weight would be enough to send her into the next world. The hospital staff said they had an infestation of lady bugs, which had somehow come in through the emergency room and were slowly moving up from floor to floor. As a room became infested, the staff emptied the room by moving patients and then sprayed—

which only managed to send the lady bugs through the ventilation up to the next floor.

"When the lady bugs reached the top floor," I asked, "would they find their way out and fly out and up toward the heavens?"

When you describe your setting, choose sensory details with an eye to how they will affect the emotional life of your characters.

Setting Worksheet

If needed, review the directions for a sensory detail worksheet. Choose one setting in your story to write about. Use notebook paper to do two sensory details worksheets, one for a reinforcing mood and one for a contrasting mood. At the top of the sensory details worksheet, I like to write the name of the mood I'm trying to evoke, such as anxious, curious, exhausted, hopeful, etc. When you have enough details on the worksheets, write your paragraphs below.

1. REINFORCE THE MOOD OF THE STORY.

2. CONTRAST WITH THE MOOD OF THE STORY.

Setting Debriefing

After working on setting, rate your strengths in these areas: 1-strong to 5-weak

Describing scenes with strong imagery_____
Using scene to affect mood_____
Are there any surprises in how well you handled setting?

LIST YOUR PRIORITIES FOR REVISION:

Group Session 6: Setting

Discuss how the setting is a frame for the actions and emotions of each story.

Mark a section of your novel where the setting works well. Share these sections.

PLAN OF ACTION:

Chapter 9
Depth

Narrative Patterning

At the 2003 SCBWI Midwinter Conference in New York City, Linda Sue Parks, author of the 2002 Newbery book, *A Single Shard*, gave the keynote speech. Parks said, "Each scene must have an element that looks back and one that looks forward. Knitting scenes together like this makes the story well integrated."

Her rule is that each element, each detail must be used at least twice in the story. Three times is better. For example, in *A Single Shard*, the story starts with rice leaking from a woven basket used as a backpack. This is repeated later when a similar backpack is used to carry the pottery to the capital city. If the element can't be repeated somewhere, Park usually omits it.

This type of narrative patterning, or knitting together of scenes, is one way of looking at the depth of a story. Depth is an unconscious search for patterns in organization, coherence, sufficiency. The sum of the parts adds up to something more—and we call that something, depth.

I see depth as connecting ideas. The easiest way to do that is to have patterns of repetition: Three (traditional European), Four (Navajo, African), seven (European), nine (three x three, European) and twelve (European). So we get the three little pigs, the seven dwarves, the twelve dancing princesses. But depth can go beyond these obvious repetitions to another level that connects ideas.

One way to connect scenes is to use a Mirror Character. This is a character who resembles another in something like attitude, upbringing, experience. They are used to highlight similarities or contrast differences.

For example in Charles Dicken's "A Christmas Story," Scrooge is mirrored by Jacob Marley, his ex-partner. What has happened to Marley will happen to Scrooge unless he changes his ways. Scrooge is also mirrored by Tiny Tim: Scrooge's temperament is shriveled, and Tiny Tim's legs are shriveled; when Scrooge's spirit heals, Tiny Tim gets well.

In the movie, *"The Pirates of the Caribbean: Curse of the Black Pearl,"* think of the two comical British soldiers which are balanced with two comical pirates.

When the writer builds in connections between plot elements or characters, the reader may be unaware of them on a conscious level. But on a sub-conscious level, the connections add up to the elusive depth.

These are the macro things that you can do to add depth. Always remember that merely adding patterns won't help add depth, if there aren't ideas to back up the patterns.

Narrative Patterning Exercise

Watch "Star Wars: The Empire Strikes Back" or "Pirates of the Caribbean: Curse of the Black Pearl" and identify as many narrative patternings as you can. The Pirate movie has delightful repetitions of dialogue that mean something different when repeated, repetition of elements, mirrors between the pirates and soldiers and much more.

1. Repeated objects. In the opening scenes of a ship wreck, an umbrella floats by. Later an umbrella used to protect pirates from moon rays that will expose them as skeletons. Elizabeth is given a dress by her father and later, she's given a dress by the pirate captain.

2. Repeated lines of dialogue mean something different with each repetition. Sometimes, dialogue is almost repeated, but with small changes: "I want a parlay."

"That's the worst pirate I've even seen./That's the best pirate I've ever seen."

3. Two scenes are repeated, but with substitutions. Early in the movie, Elizabeth is standing on the wall of the fort and falls into the water; toward the end, Captain Jack Sparrow stands in the same place and dives in.

Deeper Still: Words

We talked about connections between large story elements like scenes. Here, we'll discuss connections made by word choices.

Progressions

In my first picture book, *The River Dragon*, I had described the dragon's voice as "the clink of copper coins." Each time the dragon appeared, we heard him clinking along. The editor suggested a progression of sounds going from copper to silver to gold—with appropriate phrasing, of course. It didn't work.

Instead, I went toward baser metals: voice like the clink of copper coins, voice like the sound of a brass gong, voice ringing like a hammer on an iron anvil. This worked well because each step was a baser metal, a louder voice, and eventually, it wound up with the iron anvil, which harkened back to the main character's job as a blacksmith—which connected the sounds of the story in a different way.

Darcy Pattison

Advanced Word Banks: Imagery

When I was working on *The River Dragon*, I was also studying *How Does a Poem Mean?* by John Ciardi and Miller Williams. These poets use imagery carefully, and I hoped to learn something about language and imagery from them.

In one section, Ciardi discusses word choices in a section of John Milton's Paradise Lost. Ciardi says, (p.110): ". . . the words are being selected from inside their connotations and in answer to one another's connotations. . . ."

Ciardi looks at the connotations that connect the words of the poem. He says Milton drew upon three ideas or themes: watery motion, regal splendor, or the combination of these two. Ciardi goes into more depth and you should read it; but his example gives us a sort of mechanical way to start to enter into control of imagery. As you develop more skill, this should become internalized and become more intuitive—but for the early learning stage, let's try this.

For my picturebook, *The River Dragon*, I wanted to try this sort of control of imagery. I decided to make a list of "water verbs." It became an Imagery Word Bank from which I withdrew words whenever the dragon moved around. So, as a dragon in charge of water, he never just "flies." Here are the verbs connected to the dragon:

His tail <u>waved</u> from side to side.
He <u>surged</u> into the air.
Ti Lung <u>dove</u> under the bridge.
"Hsi! Hsi!" <u>thundered</u> the River Dragon.
Ti Lung <u>flowed</u> out from under the bridge.

In other words, connotations are speaking to connotations creating strong, connected imagery, and he has become a water dragon. Likewise, your novel is a context for making choices.

Depth Worksheet

IDENTIFY THEMES, IDEAS, OBJECTS, DIALOGUE OR OTHER ELEMENTS THAT YOU want to reinforce.

DO YOU HAVE A MIRROR CHARACTER? COULD YOU HAVE A mirror character?

ARE THERE SCENES THAT YOU WANT TO CONNECT TO CREATE A pattern? Can you connect them with any of these?

>   Scenes are repeated exactly, but with different outcomes.
>   Scenes are repeated with small changes.
>   Scenes go through the same steps but come out differently
>   Scenes go through different steps but come out similar.
>   Characters have similar counterparts.
>   Dialogue repeats exactly, but means something different each time.
>   Imagery has consistent connotations.

LOOK FOR REPETITIONS THAT ARE ALREADY THERE—what images are you unconsciously using? Do these images reinforce the themes of the story? Could the images be developed further?

ANY IDEAS FOR A WORD BANK, SUCH AS MY WATER VERBS?

ARE THERE ANY PLACES TO BUILD IN PROGRESSIONS? BAD, worse, worst/good, better, best?

. . .

DOES EACH SCENE HAVE AN ELEMENT THAT LOOKS FORWARD AND backward?

Depth Debriefing

After working on narrative patterning, rate your strengths in these areas: 1-strong to 5-weak

    Using patterns to strengthen ideas, themes, objects, etc.____
    Word progressions____
    Using imagery_____

ARE THERE ANY SURPRISES IN HOW WELL YOU HANDLED narrative patterning and imagery?

LIST YOUR PRIORITIES FOR REVISION:

Group Session 7: Depth

Discuss each novel in turn:

- Are elements and details of the story used more than once?
- Are there larger narrative patterns already present?
- Try to identify where some patterns could be established or strengthened.
- Discuss how each novel is a context for making choices about imagery.
- Read aloud sections that demonstrate good imagery. Discuss places where imagery needs to be controlled better in each novel.

Tell Better Stories for Kids

- What are some images you see in each novel?
- Are the images controlled?
- Suggestions for other images—are things happening in the novel that could be strengthened and developed into an image?

PLAN OF ACTION:

Chapter 10
Your Revision Plan

Novels are complex, yet focused, large in scope and effect, the emotional argument about ideas of great import. It makes sense that novels require revision to get the story right. In this chapter you'll plan your revision; I just need to mention a couple other things before you get busy.

Attitude Check

Revision is a dirty word. It means we must get our hands dirty as we stir up story elements. It may mean typing the entire novel over—a great revision strategy—because it lets you see every word afresh. You might even have to retype it more than once. Revision is the only way to write a great novel.

It's at this point, though, you may need encouragement. You face a long period of thinking and working with no guarantee the results will be any better. I know this pain. Every novelist understands the emotions you're feeling now.

I'm going to assign you some homework. Read *Art and Fear: Observations On the Perils (and Rewards) of Artmaking* by David

Bayles and Ted Orland. When I present this material as a Retreat, I consider this important enough that I read the first chapter to the participants. Bayles and Orland understand the fears about our work and the fears about critics reading our work. The worst thing that could happen is for you to become discouraged and quit. You must not quit! If the thought has ever crossed your mind, get Bayles' and Orland's book.

There have been many days—for example, when I got that rotten rejection on a requested revision, or the sad rejection after the editor held onto the manuscript for fourteen months—when all I could do was sit in my office and read that book and cry. And then start working again.

Weep and work; do not quit.

About Subplots

Two things generally go wrong with freshman compositions, those essays written in a beginning college writing class. The first is that the essay is unfocused: facts, opinions, statistics, and many extra words are jumbled together into an essay that says too many things, and fails to communicate a strong central idea. Novels can fall into this trap; by following the strategies suggested in this book, you can easily overcome this.

I've seen revised novels in which the language, setting, and plot were immensely improved. Yet, there was still something lacking.

The second problem with freshman essays is that they say one thing and only one thing. Repeatedly. There is no variation on the theme, no progression of ideas, no development of a wider context or understanding for the idea. Novels can fall into this trap, too. Subplots are the way out: they can give depth, provide impetus for plot, counter-point your theme, or add emphasis to any character, theme or setting.

You may need to repeat all the steps we've gone through for each subplot: What is the narrative arc of each subplot? What is the setting for each subplot? What is the obligatory scene and epiphany of each subplot? Where does each subplot intersect and feed into the main plot?

Unfocused stories will not work on any level. Single-minded stories are best suited to short stories, picture books, and perhaps some poetry.

About Voice

If you've done your revision and worked on all the aspects of novels presented here and feel confident that you're doing well in each of these areas, you need to move on and study voice. Voice is the quality of writing that comes from an individual's personality. It's your unique way of looking at characters and actions and life. The voice bibliography included in the Recommended Reading section is a place to start.

A Plan of Action

Quickly review each section, looking at the Debriefing and the Plan of Action you wrote after the Group Sessions. Write a single statement about what revisions you'll make in each of these areas; in other words, prioritize your revision.

INVENTORY: THE BIG PICTURE

PLOTTING: OBLIGATORY SCENE, NARRATIVE ARC, EPIPHANIES, Microplotting

CHARACTERS

. . .

Darcy Pattison

SENSORY DETAILS

WORD CHOICES/LANGUAGE

SETTING

NARRATIVE PATTERNING & IMAGERY

SUBPLOTS

WRITE OUT A PLAN OF REVISION THAT INCLUDES THE THREE most important things for you to rethink:

Group Session 8: Planning Your Revision

Plan to Encourage One another

Discuss ways to encourage each other during the revision process. In the Novel Revision Retreat, participants exchange SAS (self-addressed, stamped) postcards within their group. I ask them to write a note of encouragement, or what they liked best about the other person's story. Then, wait about four to six weeks—about the time it takes to get really discouraged about revising a novel—and send the postcard. Sometimes groups choose to exchange addresses or email addresses to stay connected.

Discuss each person's plan of revision. Revise your plans based on feedback from your group.

Chapter 11
Homework

Writers should always be learners. Each novel you write is a unique journey, that draws upon your skills in different orders and with different emphases. What remains stable are the strategies, the ways you approach the writing. Strong writers have a wide range of strategies to draw upon, tools that are used as the story needs.

So, I'll leave you with one more book that you should read as you're working on your revisions. For symbolism, imagery, narrative patterning and more, this is a great resource.

Foster, Thomas C. *How to Read Literature like an English Professor: A Lively and Entertaining Guide to Reading Between the Lines*. Perennial Currents.

Happy reading; happy writing; happy revising!

Chapter 12
Recommended Reading

I always wanted a writing mentor. Alas! When I first started, I didn't know anyone else who wrote. For many years I moaned about this. If only...

One day, though, I looked around my office at all the writing books shelved there. I did have mentors! Dozens of them.

For example, if I pick up *Characters and Viewpoint* by Orson Scott Card, I remember his advice about deciding what type of story you're writing. He uses the MICE Quotient: milieu, idea, character, event. Deciding what type of story you're writing helps you decide how to characterize appropriately.

Remember the stages of learning? If you learn that you are weak in dialogue, one of the best revision strategies is to find a mentor; for most of us, that means you should find a how-to book on dialogue.

When I recommend a book here, it's because they are books I've personally read and found useful. The annotations are meant to help you decide if you will find it useful. These are opinionated annotations: sometimes, I'll recommend reading just one chapter; sometimes, I'll recommend one book by an author, but tell you to shy away from other books by the same author. This list is provided as a starting for finding your own mentors.

Happy reading!

Introductory Reading

This book assumes that you have some basic competencies. These books are an excellent review of these competencies. When I do a Novel Revision Retreat, participants are asked to read these as homework before attending. If you can master what these two books discuss, your manuscripts will get you into the top 1% of the stories written. It's getting into the top .001% of manuscripts that actually get published that the rest of this book is about.

BROWNE, RENNI AND DAVE KING. *SELF EDITING FOR FICTION WRITERS*. New York: HarperPerennial, 1993.

LUKEMAN, NOAH. *THE FIRST FIVE PAGES*. NEW YORK: FIRESIDE, Simon & Schuster,

Scenes

BICKHAM, JACK M. *SCENE AND STRUCTURE*. Cincinnati: Writer's Digest Books.

A very structured approach to plotting that is interesting to read once, but be warned that it is SO structured. However, he has a fascinating "Scenic Master Plot" in the appendix that helped me understand the flow of events across a novel, and what considerations you need to keep in mind. Great for getting a grasp on the Big Picture. This book and Sandra Scofield's book listed below have complimentary information, but their approaches are different; Scofield's book helped me actually write differently, but after reading hers, I came back to Bickham with a better appreciation of the complexities and variations of scenes that he lays out. For example, he goes into greater detail about interrupted scenes, tricks to control pacing, variations in internal structure of a scene, etc. Read Scofield and do her exercises; then read Bickham.

SCOFIELD, SANDRA. THE SCENE BOOK: A PRIMER FOR THE FICTION WRITER. New York: Penguin, 2007.

Scofield grabbed me when she described a story as simply a "rosary of scenes." This book is just fun to read. Great suggestions on exercises and self-study. Scofield says that you can make the most improvement in your stories if you just learn to write with scenes. While she includes mostly adult novels and short stories as example, she also recommends some novels for young adults and middle graders: the Newbery Honor book by Gary D. Schmidt, *Lizzie Bright and the Buckminster Boy* and the Newbery book by Karen Cushman, *Catherine, Called Birdy*.

Plotting

JAUSS, DAVID. SOME EPIPHANIES ABOUT EPIPHANIES. *The Writer's Chronicle*: A Publication of the Associated Writing Programs, October/November, 2001, Volume 32, Number 2, pp. 37-49

Good article on epiphanies, a topic that is often slighted.

KLEIN, CHERYL. SECOND SIGHT: AN EDITOR'S TALKS ON WRITING, REVISING AND PUBLISHING BOOKS FOR CHILDREN AND YOUNG ADULTS. New York: Asterisk Press,Klein is the American editor of the Harry Potter series and this is an edited collection on her presentations and speeches over several years. A good resource for many areas of revision.

. . .

MORREL, DAVID. *LESSONS FROM A LIFETIME OF WRITING*. Cincinnati : Writer's Digest Books, 2001.

Morrell is the author of First Blood, the Rambo story. I recently tried to read that book, but couldn't finish it. After all, it was Morrell's first novel, and that shows. Since then, I've read a couple of his thrillers and enjoyed them immensely. I saw him at a workshop in New Mexico and this writing teacher and master of over thirty novels has much to teach us about emotional honesty and life in general. Lesson Six has interesting strategies for dealing with very long novels. Great to read and re-read if you're struggling to pick up the pace and make sure that a reader doesn't put your story down and never return.

MORRELL, JESSICA PAGE. *THANKS, BUT THIS ISN'T FOR US: A (SORT OF) COMPASSIONATE BUIDE TO WHY YOUR WRITING IS BEING REJECTED*. New York: Jeremy P. Tharcher/Penguin, 2009.

Another good overall resource for revising.

TOBIAS, RONALD B. *20 MASTER PLOTS (AND HOW TO BUILD THEM)*. Cincinnati: Writer's Digest Books, 1993

Some say there are only two plots in the world: a stranger comes to town, or a character leaves home on a journey. Others say there are thirty basic plots. Tobias takes twenty of the most popular and culturally relevant plots and discusses typical ways they play out in today's stories. It's a great starting place for a first draft or for a major revision, helping the writer decide the general plot category for a story, the conventions of that plot structure and how the writer might break out and be original. I refer to this at least once for every story I write as a way to keep me focused.

VOGLER, CHRISTOPHER. *THE WRITER'S JOURNEY: MYTHIC*

STRUCTURE FOR WRITERS, 3rd edition. Los Angeles: Michael Weise Productions, 1998.

Vogler takes Joseph Campbell's work on the hero's myth and turns it into a tool for plot and character. If you are writing fantasy, this book is a must. But for other genres, it's extremely helpful for laying out typical plot elements, the range of appropriate plot elements at each stage of the story, and how to make sure the climax (both internal and external) are fully realized. It's one of my favorite books on writing—I've practically got it memorized.

VORHAUS, JOHN. *THE COMIC TOOLBOX: HOW TO BE FUNNY EVEN IF YOU'RE NOT*. Los Angeles: Silman-James Press, 1994.

Vorhaus has a variation of the hero's myth and lots of character stuff. Oh, yeah. He does talk about how to be funny, too, but that's not the main reason I recommend the book. Get it for character and plot.

ZUCKERMAN, ALBERT. *WRITING THE BLOCKBUSTER NOVEL*. Cincinnati: Writer's Digest Books, 2002

This is a classic book about taking stories to a deeper level and developing a story with broad appeal. It has an excellent discussion of plotting in chapters 8-12, plus a look at how a story changes and grows into a story with more emotional strength.

Character

BALLON, RACHEL, PH.D. *BREATHING LIFE INTO YOUR CHARACTERS*. Cincinnati, Ohio: Writer's Digest Books. 2003.

Ballon, a psychologist and writing coach, encourages you to look within for character motivation. I don't use this often, but sometimes it's helpful to think about how my life is coming out in this story.

. . .

CHIARELLA, TOM. *WRITING DIALOGUE*. 1998. CINCINNATI, Ohio: Story Press

This is the best resource I've found on dialogue and how to tighten it, pitfalls to avoid, and nuts and bolts such as speech tags. Lots of great suggestions. For example, he suggests that you record dialogue around you for a day. That's a revealing exercise. One valuable exercise is his compressed dialogue, where he asks you to give characters only five words at a time.

DUNNE, PETER. *EMOTIONAL STRUCTURE: CREATING THE STORY BENEATH THE PLOT, A GUIDE FOR SCREENWRITERS*. Sanger, CA: Quill Driver Books/Word Dancer Press, 2007.

Seldom do any how-to books tackle the difficult subject of the emotional arc of a story. Although this is directed at screenwriters, Dunne's book is valuable for any storyteller. He asks writers to plan scenes in a story with index cards. One side is for the plot or action of a scene and the opposite is for the emotions of the scene. By directly addressing this issue, he make it accessible and open for conscious revision.

HOOD, ANN. *CREATING CHARACTER EMOTIONS*. CINCINNATI, Ohio: Story Press. The inner life of a character brings him or her to life. Avoid cliched expressions of emotion by checking it against Hood's collection of emotional outpourings. Although she doesn't cover every emotion I need, I especially like the contrast of the cliched versions and the quoted versions. It tells me what to avoid and what to reach for. My only complaint is that the book is too short: I have started jotting emotions in the margins of the Table of Contents that I wish she had covered.

. . .

SEGER, LINDA. *CREATING UNFORGETTABLE CHARACTERS*. New York, NY: Henry Holt and Company. 1990.

So many of the great resources come from the world of screenwriting! This one is excellent, especially Chapter 5, "Creating Character Relationships." It helps you set up supporting characters who will help force that emotional arc to be dynamic.

STEIN, SOL. CHAPTER 11 IN *STEIN ON WRITING*. New York, NY: St. Martin's Press

Stein is a great resource in many ways. Sometimes, he just says things in a different way and that's helpful. But he also includes great exercises. For example, the Billfold Exercise asks you to think about what secret does your character hide in his billfold.

RISO, DON RICHARDSON WITH RUSS HUDSON. *PERSONALITY TYPES: USING THE ENNEAGRAM FOR SELF-DISCOVERY*. Boston, Massachusetts: Houghton Mifflin

An off-beat way of looking at personalities. I like it because it categorizes people by how they cope with the stresses of the world, rather than the roles they play in life. Takes a bit of reading to understand, but it's fun.

LAUTHRE, HOWARD. *CREATING CHARACTERS: A WRITER'S REFERENCE TO THE PERSONALITY TRAITS THAT BRING FICTIONAL PEOPLE TO LIFE*. Jefferson, N. Carolina: McFarland, 1998.

Great resource for creating unique characters. This book has encyclopedic lists of internal and external traits, characters like or dislikes, strengths or weaknesses, and much more. When you first start a novel or a revision, it's great to flip through this book for possibilities.

Language

Most of the exercises focused word usage, but there are many other areas of style and language that could and should be explored in your writing. These titles will give you a start.

LE GUIN, URSULA K. *STEERING THE CRAFT*. PORTLAND: THE Eighth Mountain Press.

A master at the craft of writing, Le Guin offers exercises on "sounding gorgeous," punctuation, long and short sentences, and much more. Perfect for use in a group, these exercises will stretch your writing skills—always a good thing! After doing one of her exercises, I wrote my first really long sentence.

HICKEY, DONA J. *DEVELOPING A WRITTEN VOICE*. MOUNTAIN View, California: Mayfield Publishing Company, 1993.

Though this is meant to be used in more academic settings, Hickey has intriguing exercises that encourage writers to experiment with different voices. Wow! If you try a couple of these, what a difference it makes in your understanding of your options to create voice. Hickey tackles subjects about voice that no one else dares.

DICTIONARIES. YOU SHOULD PURCHASE A GOOD UNABRIDGED dictionary for your writing office. Try to find one that indicates the origin of words, as that will help you more carefully locate the connotations of words.

LONGKNIFE, ANN AND K.D. SULLIVAN. *THE ART OF STYLING SENTENCES*. New York: Barrons Educational Press, 2002.

Writers should be the masters of their sentences. Do you know how to interrupt a sentence with another sentence and correctly punctuate it? Are you comfortable using colons and semi-colons? If you need a brush-up on punctuation for complex sentences, if you want to learn how to vary sentence structure, if you want to play with words, then try this book.

WILLIAMS, JOSEPH. *STYLE: TOWARD CLARITY AND GRACE*. Chicago: The University of Chicago Press, 1990.
   Though this book is most helpful for non-fiction writers, fiction writers can learn much here about clarity, concision, emphasis, coherence and elegance. Williams structured approach is easy to follow and has interesting examples. Every writer should read through his book at least once.

Sensory Details

BROWN, DAVE AND RENNI KING. *SELF-EDITING FOR FICTION WRITERS*, New York: HarperPerennial, 1993
   Yes, this book is useful for several areas. It reinforces everything said here about using sensory details to Show-Don't-Tell, and much more. Easy exercises demonstrate each chapter.

LUKEMAN, NOAH. *THE FIRST FIVE PAGES*. NEW YORK: A Fireside Book, Simon & Schuster, 2000.
   Likewise Lukeman emphasizes the importance of sensory details in Show-don't-Tell. If the first five pages don't show specific details, you've lost the editor's attention. Re-read Chapter 2 and 11 for this section.

STEIN, SOL. *STEIN ON WRITING*. NEW YORK: ST. MARTIN'S Press, 1995.

Stein is a great resource in many ways. Sometimes, he just says things in a different way and that's helpful. But he also includes great exercises. For example, the Billfold Exercise asks you to think about what secret does your character hide in his billfold. Chapter 12 is a good overview of Show-Don't-Tell.

Ackerman, Diane. *A Natural History of the Senses*. New York: Vintage Books, a Division of Random House, 1990.

Known for her excellent non-fiction, Diane Ackerman provides a thorough look at the world of the senses. I learned fascinating tidbits by reading this book, but more important, I appreciate the "sense-lucious world" in which we live and the importance of including those sensory details in fiction. This is one book every writer should read.

Setting

Noble, William. *Three Rules for Writing a Novel: A Guide to Story Development*. Forest Dale, Vermont: Paul S. Eriksson, 1997.

This is a compilation of three of Noble's previous books about writing. You want to focus on the "Where Am I?" section (which was previously published as Make That Scene), which concentrates on setting, especially

Depth

As important as this topic is to creating stories of depth, there isn't much written about it. There are chapters here and there, and that's the best I can find.

. . .

Tell Better Stories for Kids

CIARDI, JOHN AND JOSEPH HARRISS, *HOW DOES A POEM MEAN?* Boston, Massachusetts: Houghton Mifflin, 1990. (Or try the earlier version edited with Miller Williams)

Poets know words: Ciardi explains words better than anyone I've read how to use the connotations of words to create meaning. Along with the use of sensory details, this is the path toward "Show Don't Tell." You'll probably have to get this one at a used book store, but it's well worth the effort. Because I'm not a poet, it took me a year to read through the entire book but it has stayed with me in so many ways.

DIBBELL, ANSEN. *PLOT.* CINCINNATI: WRITERS DIGEST BOOKS, 1999.

I don't recommend this book for plot, because it doesn't add much to the conversation that you can't find better discussed elsewhere. But Dibbell has one of the few discussions of narrative patterning that you'll find. Read Chapter 5, especially about parallel plotlines, and Chapter 8 about patterns, mirrors, and echoes.

FOSTER, THOMAS C. *HOW TO READ LITERATURE LIKE AN ENGLISH PROFESSOR: A LIVELY AND ENTERTAINING GUIDE TO READING BETWEEN THE LINES.* Perennial Currents. 2003.

For symbolism, imagery, narrative patterning and more, this is a great resource. Read this one as you work on your revisions.

GERARD, PHILLIP. *WRITING A BOOK THAT MAKES A DIFFERENCE.* Cincinnati: Story Press, 2000.

Always wanted to leave your mark on the world? Gerard encourages you to tackle the big topics that scare you. Here, though, I recommend reading Chapter 6 for ways of developing theme through narrative patterning.

. . .

LeGuin, Ursula K. *The Wave in the Mind*. Boston: Shambhala Publications.

LeGuin's collection of essays here is uneven, with some interesting and others less so. Read "Stress-Rhythm in Poetry and Prose" and "Rhythmic Pattern in The Lord of the Rings." LeGuin does a great job of illustrating narrative patterning in this popular novel.

Prose, Francine. *Reading Like a Writer: A Guide for People Who Love Books and for Those Who Want to Write Them*. New York: Harpercollins, 2006.

This is an interesting book, which approaches reading as a writer. Yes, as a writer I read differently than I used to. Seldom does a story sweep me away into a new world. I might get caught up for a while, but at some point, I stop and admire the writer's technique. Prose discusses ways writers can learn by careful reading. Great chapters on the way writers tie stories together with patterns.

Voice

Basic Competencies

I've discussed these before. If you didn't follow my advice and read them before you started your revision, read them now!

Browne, Renni and Dave King. *Self Editing for Fiction Writers*. New York: HarperPerennial, 1993

Lukeman, Noah. *The First Five Pages*. New York: Fireside, Simon & Schuster, 2000.

Tell Better Stories for Kids

Language and Style Issues

Most of the language exercises in this book focus on word usage, but other areas of style and language could and should be explored in your writing. These titles will give you a start.

CIARDI, JOHN AND JOSEPH HARRISS. *HOW DOES A POEM MEAN?* Boston, MA: Houghton Mifflin, 1990. (Or the earlier version edited with Miller Williams)

Poets know words: Ciardi explains better than anyone I've read how to use the connotations of words to create meaning. Along with the use of sensory details, this is the path toward "Show Don't Tell."

DICTIONARIES. YOU SHOULD PURCHASE A GOOD UNABRIDGED dictionary for your writing office. Try to find one that indicates the origin of words, as that will help you more carefully locate the connotations of words.

GLASER, JOE. *UNDERSTANDING STYLE: PRACTICAL WAYS TO IMPROVE YOUR WRITING*. New York: Oxford University Press, 1999.

Take the mystery out of style with lots of exercises to practice.

GORDON, KAREN ELIZABETH. *THE NEW WELL-TEMPERED SENTENCE: A PUNCTUATION HANDBOOK FOR THE INNOCENT, THE EAGER, AND THE DOOMED*. New York: Ticknor & Fields, 1993.

Sentences with an attitude.

HALE, CONSTANCE. *SIN AND SYNTAX: HOW TO CRAFT WICKEDLY EFFECTIVE PROSE*. New York: Broadway Books, 2001.

Good examples of how grammar affects meaning.

. . .

HICKEY, DONA J. *DEVELOPING A WRITTEN VOICE.* MOUNTAIN View, California: Mayfield Publishing Company, 1993.

Though this is meant to be used in more academic settings, Hickey has intriguing exercises that encourage writers to experiment with different voices. Along with LeGuin's book, it's my favorite on voice.

LE GUIN, URSULA K. *STEERING THE CRAFT.* PORTLAND: The Eighth Mountain Press.

A master at the craft of writing, Le Guin offers exercises on "sounding gorgeous," punctuation, long and short sentences, and much more. Perfect for use in a group, these exercises will stretch your writing skills—always a good thing! After doing one of her exercises, I wrote my first really long sentence. I still challenge myself to write one very long sentence in every novel.

LONGKNIFE, ANN AND K.D. SULLIVAN. *THE ART OF STYLING SENTENCES.* New York: Barrons Educational Press, 2002.

If you need a brush-up on punctuation for complex sentences, if you want to learn how to vary sentence structure, if you want to play with words, then try this book. Every writer should have control of their language and controlling sentences is a good place to begin.

YOLEN, JANE. *TAKE JOY: THE WRITER'S GUIDE TO LOVING THE CRAFT.* Writer's Digest Books, 2007.

Great chapter on finding your voice v. creating voice for a particular story.

. . .

WILLIAMS, JOSEPH. *STYLE: TOWARD CLARITY AND GRACE*. Chicago: The University of Chicago Press, 1990.

Though this book is most helpful for non-fiction writers, fiction writers can learn much here about clarity, concision, emphasis, coherence and elegance.

The Writing Life

BAYLES, DAVID AND TED ORLAND. *ART & FEAR: OBSERVATIONS ON THE PERILS (AND REWARDS) OF ARTMAKING*. Santa Barbara, California: Capra Press, 1993.

When fears about your work overwhelm you, read this book. Do not quit working! Read this book. There have been days, after a disappointing rejection, all I could do was cry and re-read this book. It reminds me that art is made by flawed people.

Chapter 13
APPENDIX A: I Don't Want an Honest Critique

No, don't tell me what's wrong with this novel. I don't want to hear it. Minor problems? OK, I'll fix those. But major structural, plot or character problems—don't tell me.

Cynthia Ozynick says, "Writing is essentially an act of courage." When I get an honest critique, my courage fails me. I fear the revision needed: I won't ever be able to "get it right." Obviously, I thought that I had communicated my intentions well in the first draft, or I would have changed it before you read it. But you say that you don't understand, or that I'm inconsistent, or that I'm unfocused. How could that be? I see it so clearly. And if my vision of my story is so skewed, then how will I ever get it right?

I fear that you're right and I'm wrong. But how can I be sure? This is my story and it comes from my psychological leanings, my background, my research. How can you tell me what is right for my story? If the story doesn't communicate what I want, then, yes, I need to revise. I repeat: Obviously, I thought it did communicate what I wanted, or I would have revised it before you saw it. Do you just have a different vision of the story because of your psychological leanings, your background? Are you trying to envision what I intended, or are you envisioning what you would have written? Where does your ego slam up against my ego? And where does your objective appraisal need to push my ego back into line with what it really wants to do anyway? Perspective is hard to achieve.

I fear that all my hard work—all the months spent thinking and rewriting—will be wasted. As a novelist, time haunts me. To write a novel isn't the work of a week or a month. It takes many months, a year, a year and a half. More. It's a long, long process. Your revision notes mean that the time is extended, and that without any guarantee of being finished even then. Meanwhile, that means that I'm a year older, that it's a year in which I couldn't write anything new (even if I could find the courage to begin again). I fear your honesty; I need your approval (or someone's approval; if not yours, then whose?). Will it crush me emotionally if you don't "like" my story? I gloss over the approval part of critiques and agonize over the "needs work" assessment. Is there a way for you to only show approval, yet open my eyes, so that I recognize what needs work? I'd rather recognize it for myself than have it pointed out.

I fear that my standards are too lax. I want to be finished, I want to have this story out there. I want to have written, but in the throes of writing, I want the end of the process long before the story is really finished. Submission comes too early and then I get rejections. Then, it's harder than ever to revise. But waiting is excruciating. Typical advice: Put the manuscript in a drawer for three months and then pull it out and read it with a fresh eye. What? Waste three more months? Never. It's done and ready to send out. (Ok, maybe it isn't, but I can't stand looking at it one more time and in three months, my editor could read it and buy it. OK, maybe they won't buy it until I revise, but three months? Isn't there any other way?)

Critiques, especially honest and on-target critiques, are fearful things. I know that I need them; but they are painful, emotionally draining, and confidence shaking. But I need them. OK, can you give me a minute? Let me find my mask of courage. There. I have it on. Now bring on your best critique!

Top 10 Ways to Stop the Sting of Critiques

1. Avoidance. Have someone else read the critique for you and only highlight the good comments. Read only the highlighted comments.

2. Revenge. Give the creep back an even harsher critique than you just got.

3. Denial. Write out the reasons why the critiquer is totally off base. Ignore all suggestions.

4. Excitement. Fake excitement about the critique and tell everyone you know exactly what's wrong with the story and how you plan to fix it.

5. Suspicion. Read each comment with the suspicion that the critiquer is trying to get your manuscript out of the running, so their own manuscript will do well. Therefore, you can safely ignore any comments you want to.

6. Surprise. Allow each comment to be a revelation at how far off base this critiquer is.

7. Pride. Take pride in your ability to "take it" from the tough ones.

8. Loneliness. Understand that you and you alone are in the situation of receiving harsh critiques; such things have never been written about any manuscript and will never be written again.

9. Forgiveness. Realize that the critiquer has sinned by so harshly criticizing your story and at some point they will have to come and ask for forgiveness; be ready to give it gracefully.

10. Hope. Find hope in the good things the critiquer noticed, and hope in the process of revision.

Chapter 14
APPENDIX B: Group Manuscript Evaluation Form

Use this form to evaluate manuscripts from others in your group before you come to the retreat.

(Permission granted to photocopy this page as needed.)

Author:
Title:

AS YOU READ THE NOVELS OF OTHERS IN YOUR GROUP, JOT NOTES here. Don't worry about line editing. Enjoy the novel! Mark any major points you want to discuss, as well as the points below.

As you read, note the following in the manuscript.

1. FIVE STRONGEST CHAPTERS/FIVE WEAKEST CHAPTERS.

2. HIGHLIGHT A STRONG EXAMPLE OF CHARACTERIZATION.

3. Highlight a strong example of use of language.

4. Highlight a strong example of setting.

5. Think about the overall plot. Does it build to a satisfying climax? In a short paragraph, summarize the plot.

6. Summarize the story in one sentence.

About the Author

Children's book author and indie publisher Darcy Pattison writes award-winning fiction and non-fiction books for children. Her works have received starred PW, Kirkus, and BCCB reviews. Awards include the Irma Black Honor award, six NSTA Outstanding Science Trade Books, six Eureka! Nonfiction Honor book, two Junior Library Guild selections, two NCTE Notable Children's Book in Language Arts, a Notable Social Studies Trade Books, a NSTA Best STEM book, and an Arkansiana Award. She's the 2007 recipient of the Arkansas Governor's Arts Award for Individual Artist for her work in children's literature. Her works are translated into eleven languages.

Always active, before her tenth birthday, she (almost) climbed the Continental Divide, turning back at the last twenty yards because it was too steep and great climbing shoes hadn't been invented yet. She once rode a bicycle down a volcano in Bali, Indonesia and has often hiked the Rockies. She's hiked New Zealand's backcountry for a taste of Kiwi life, and then strolled the beaches of Australia. In 2024, she (finally) climbed the 14,043 foot Mt. Sherman in Colorado—hurrah for great hiking shoes. On her bucket list is kayaking the Nā Pali Coast of Hawaii and eating curry in Mumbai.

For Darcy's books, see MimsHouseBooks.com

www.ingramcontent.com/pod-product-compliance
Lightning Source LLC
Chambersburg PA
CBHW031156020426
42333CB00013B/697